The Creoles of Color
of New Orleans

The Creoles of Color
of New Orleans

By James Haskins

Drawings by Don Miller

Thomas Y. Crowell Company   New York

Acknowledgment is made to the following for permission to use copyrighted material:

Quadrangle/The New York Times Book Co., American Negro Folklore *by J. Mason Brewer; copyright © 1968.*

Houghton Mifflin Company, Leaves from the Diary of an Impressionist *by Lafcadio Hearn; copyright © 1911.*

Library of Congress Cataloging in Publication Data
Haskins, James, 1941–   The Creoles of color of New Orleans.

SUMMARY: Traces the history of the group of people in New Orleans who are "of mixed Spanish or French and African or West Indian blood."   Bibliography: p.   1. Creoles—Juv. lit. 2. New Orleans—History—Juv. lit. [1. Creoles. 2. New Orleans—History] I. Miller, Don, illus. II. Title. F379.N59C873   917.63'35   74-12487
ISBN 0-690-00224-6

1   2   3   4   5   6   7   8   9   10

To Cathy

By the Author

Diary of a Harlem Schoolteacher
Resistance: *Profiles in Nonviolence*
Revolutionaries: *Agents of Change*
The War and the Protest: *Vietnam*
Profiles in Black Power
A Piece of the Power: *Four Black Mayors*
From Lew Alcindor to Kareem Abdul Jabbar
Religions
The Psychology of Black Language, with Hugh F. Butts, M.D.
Black Manifesto for Education (editor)
Jokes from Black Folks
Adam Clayton Powell: *Portrait of a Marching Black*
Pinckney Benton Stewart Pinchback: *A Biography*
Street Gangs Yesterday and Today
Witchcraft, Mysticism and Magic in the Black World
Ralph Bunche: *A Most Reluctant Hero*
Babe Ruth and Hank Aaron: *The Home Run Kings*
Snow Sculpture and Ice Carving: *The Art of Creating Transient
   Forms*

Acknowledgments

Without the help of the following librarians, who freely gave of their time and assistance in making available to me the many disparate resources on the Creoles of color in New Orleans, this book could never have become a reality: Susan Birenbaum, Fine Arts Librarian, Tulane University Library, New Orleans; Collin B. Hamer, Jr., Head of the Louisiana Division, City of New Orleans Public Library; Don P. Morrison, Head of the Photo Duplications Department, Louisiana State University Library, Baton Rouge; Peggy Richards, Director, Louisiana State Museum, New Orleans; Ruth Ann Stewart, Assistant Curator of the Schomburg Collection, New York City; and Paul Wank, Information Librarian, Louisiana State University Library, Baton Rouge.

Grateful thanks are due also to my editors, Ann Beneduce and Virginia Buckley, for their great patience; to Mary Ellen Arrington, Vivian Levy, and Virginia Wright, for their help in researching the book; to Mary Ellen Agolia and Mary Ellen Arrington, who typed the manuscript drafts; and to Kathy Benson, who helped to pull it all together.

Finally, a very special acknowledgment to Roland Wingfield, who, as a candidate for a master of arts degree from Louisiana State University in 1961, wrote the most informative and inclusive study of the Creoles of color in New Orleans that currently exists. Without this valuable study, the story of the Creoles of color after the close of the nineteenth century would have been incomplete.

Contents

Introduction

Who are the Creoles of color? Three Louisiana writers, or historians, will give three different answers. One will say, "There are no Creoles of color; there are only white Creoles, the descendants of the first French and Spanish settlers." Another will say, "Anyone or anything native to Louisiana can be called Creole; a Creole does not even have to have French or Spanish ancestors." Still another will say, "The Creoles of color are a class of people of mixed Spanish or French and African or West Indian blood whose families have been free for generations. Their culture and language were French, as were the culture and language of most of the white settlers, although now all groups in New Orleans are Americanized." Today, the majority of Americans agree with the last definition, and it is the definition that is used in this book. But what to call this group of people is not as important as their history and their way of life today.

The story of New Orleans is filled with references to this free colored group—fascinating references to their customs and to their changing social situation, for there were times when they enjoyed a privileged status and other times when they suffered great discrimination. Throughout their history they have insisted upon being a separate class: proud of their long-time freedom, proud of their French culture, more resistant to change and Americanization than any other group living in New Orleans when the United States purchased the Louisiana Territory in 1803. No account of New Orleans up to the twentieth century fails to mention this class of free colored people. Twentieth-century New Orleans history is a different matter. Very little has been written about the Creoles of today, which is unfortunate, for it is interesting to see how their life and culture have changed in this century: to what degree they have been assimilated, what customs and traditions they have maintained, and how they have helped New Orleans to remain, even today, the most "foreign" city in the United States.

This book is written in three parts. The first tells the story of New Orleans from its founding by the French early in the 1700s to the rise of the Creoles, and relates their history in the eighteenth and nine-teenth centuries.

With the coming of the twentieth century, the

Creoles began to change. Partly this change was due to the great discrimination they faced when the South passed laws segregating all people of color in nearly every area of life. The change was due mostly, though, to the increasing Americanization of New Orleans—to the technological advances of industry, the "progress" that is gradually causing every distinct group of people in the country to become less and less different from other Americans. The second section tells about these changes.

The third section of the book tells about some of the contributions that the Creoles have made to New Orleans and American life and culture. Other contributions are mentioned elsewhere in the book. Altogether, the three sections are meant to introduce the reader to the Creoles of color, one of the unique groups of people living in the United States today, and to bring together their history, past and present, before they, like so many other groups, "melt" into the mainstream of American life and culture.

SECTION I
Old Creole Days

CHAPTER 1

The French Settle in New Orleans

The Old City murmurs: Rest with me. I am old, but thou hast never met with a younger more beautiful than I. I dwell in eternal summer, I dream in perennial sunshine, I sleep in magical moonlight. My streets are flecked, with strange, sharp shadows, and sometimes also the Shadow of Death falls upon them, but if thou wilt not fear, thou art safe. My charms are not the charms of much gold and great riches, but thou mayst feel with me such hope and content as thou hast never felt before. I offer thee eternal summer, a sky divinely blue; sweet breezes and sweet perfumes, bright fruits and flowers fairer than the rainbow. Rest with me. For if thou leavest me, thou must forever remember me with regret.[1]

The author of these words, Lafcadio Hearn, was writing about a section of New Orleans, Louisiana, in 1911. The section, known as the French Quarter or the Old City, was old then, and it is older today. But today, as then, it is still young. Once, the Old City section made up the entire area of New Orleans. Now, it is only a small part of a large modern city; but even a visitor somehow knows that the heart and soul of New Orleans do not lie in the steel and glass and noise and clamor of the larger metropolis, but in the mysterious, strangely shaped buildings and shadowed streets and timeless silence of the Old City.

Walk into the Old City. The buildings are unlike any others: bright yellow, deep sea-green, brick-red, dull pink, blue, chocolate, blazing white—all trimmed with the bright green of the old iron balconies, some two or three stories high, curving and swirling, no two patterns the same. There are balconies everywhere, and stairways that leap from building to building, and curious covered bridges, and little alleyways piercing from one street to another, and old window shutters folded back against the walls. Plaster peels, crumbles, and falls from the stout pillars of the arcades, and the little patios are sometimes overrun with once well-kept gardens gone wild. But one does not feel that the Old City is really old—just dozing peacefully in the early morning sun. Any moment it might awaken, yawn and stretch, and with a smile become the bustling little town that was once the most foreign place in America. If you walk down that dark little alleyway, the one with sunlight at the other end, maybe you will emerge into the city of nearly a century ago . . .

It is early morning, but already the streets are alive with activity. The street vendors are out, peddling their wares. The grits man announces his presence with a long-drawn-out tooting of his great tin horn; the hooves of his horse and the iron wheels of his little covered wagon clop-clop and rumble along the cobble-stoned streets. *"Belle fromage!"* cries the cream-and-cheese woman, laden with her baskets of cheeses and cans of fresh cream. *"Belles saucisses!" "Belle chaurice!"* announce the sausage men with assurance, for they know their delicious meats will all be sold. *"Belle cala! Tout chaud!"* rings through the morning air, and the old black *cala* woman gestures toward her cart laden with delicious rice cakes, piping hot for breakfast. Creole servant women emerge from the doors of nearby houses to buy the street vendors' wares and to stand talking for a moment in the morning sun.

Although it is still early morning, the women

have been busy. They have carefully parched beans of green coffee to a rich brown, ground them in the coffee mill, and then poured boiling water slowly over them for that first morning cup of coffee which the old people say is the secret to long life. They have already set out the herbs and spices for making the main meal: the gombo or the jambalaya or the crawfish bisque. Later they will go to the Marché St. Bernard for vegetables and meat or fish.

In many kitchens the dish to be prepared is a fish soup called court bouillon, and it will be prepared with special pride. Even today, New Orleans court bouillon is regarded as a soup with a special history, for it contains something from almost every group of people who have lived in New Orleans—something from the Indians, something from the Spaniards, something from the French, perhaps even something from the American settlers; and certainly something important from the Creoles of color. It was these Creoles—a mixture of the blood of the African slaves with that of the French who founded New Orleans, and with perhaps the blood of the Indians who first inhabited the area now called Louisiana, or with that of the Spaniards who ruled Louisiana for a time and gave New Orleans its beautiful architecture, or with that of the Santo Domingans who fled to New Orleans from the revolution in their island home (which was renamed Haiti as a result)—who brought all the ingredients together to make the delicious court bouillon. Yes, court bouillon is a mixture created by many peoples—and the Creoles, too, are a combination of different peoples. New Orleans is the city with the greatest variety of people and cooking in the United States. Perhaps that is why, even today, New Orleans is such an exciting place and why its inhabitants enjoy a specialness unknown to people anywhere else. The story of the city and its unique people, the Creoles, is a fascinating one.

The tale begins with the Mississippi River. The Spanish called it at first a name meaning "River of the Holy Ghost," then "Rio Escondido" and "Rio Grande." The French called it "St. Louis," "Colbert," and "La Palisade." The Algonquin Indians in the East called it "Me-ac-cha-sippi," which means "Father of the Waters." After a while that's what everyone called it, which was right because, after all, the Indians were the first to know about the Mississippi. But the Indians did not have it to themselves once others discovered it.

The Spaniards were the first Europeans to discover the Mississippi. They sailed down the river in the early 1500s. But they staked no claims and established no settlements. They were looking for the gold and silver and jewels that they had heard abounded in "Florida," by which name the North American mainland was known. The most famous of

these men was Hernando de Soto. In the spring of
1541 he and his men crossed the Mississippi in their
search for riches; they returned, discouraged, to the
river many months later. There De Soto died. He was
buried in the Mississippi itself, for he and his men
had angered the Indians, and his men were afraid the
Indians would desecrate his body if they found it.
Later, De Soto's men went west again, across the Red
River into Texas. But still they found no riches, and
they returned to the Mississippi once more and
followed it to the sea.

Although these Spaniards had traveled along the
Mississippi, their reason for being there was their
quest for wealth. They did not take particular note
either of the river or of the land on either side of it. In
fact, when the Frenchman Robert Cavelier, better
known as La Salle, reached the end of the great
waterway in 1682, he did not even know that Spanish
explorers had gone down the lower Mississippi. La
Salle did know that other Frenchmen, notably Mar-
quette, had traveled the river, so he gave the land
surrounding it a French name. He named the land
Louisiana, in honor of his king, Louis XIV.

The French were enemies of the Spanish, and La
Salle quickly saw that a settlement at the mouth of
the great river would be a good launching point for
attack forces to bother the Spanish in Mexico. He
asked King Louis's permission to build such a

settlement, and received that permission. In 1684, he sailed to Louisiana with several hundred colonists. But somehow, their ships missed the mouth of the Mississippi and landed in Texas instead. The settlement they tried to establish there was a failure, and La Salle was killed by his own men.

After the death of La Salle, Louisiana saw few Frenchmen for many years. Some French trappers and traders moved through the territory, but the king of France was not interested in it. Then, in 1697, King Louis turned his attention to Louisiana once again. The English had already colonized much of the eastern part of North America and had been at war with the French for Canada for many years. King Louis saw Louisiana as an additional French outpost in North America to prevent the British from acquiring too much territory on the continent.

Pierre Le Moyne, usually called Iberville, was soon sent to establish a settlement in Louisiana before the English could do so. His ship entered the Mississippi on March 3, 1699. It was late in the day, and when the ship reached the first great bend in the river, Iberville ordered the anchor dropped. The party would camp for the night on the right bank of the river and continue their journey the next day. While his men set up camp, Iberville walked along the river bank, thinking how far away they were from France. Suddenly he remembered that in France this day was

Mardi Gras—the day of the carnival festival before
Ash Wednesday, when the people enjoyed their last
celebration before Lent began. Looking around him,
Iberville decided to name the place of encampment
"Mardi Gras."

Iberville and his crew continued along the Mississippi. Finally, he decided on a spot in a wooded
area near the mouth of the river for establishing the
settlement. A year later his men built the little Fort de
Mississippi there.

France's interest in Louisiana now was increasing, and it was decided that a larger town should be
built. Many miles above Fort de Mississippi the river
curved out and around in a crescent shape; Iberville
had thought it one of the most beautiful parts of the
river, and it was within this curve that New Orleans
was built. Work was begun on the settlement in the
early spring of 1718, twelve years after Iberville's
death.

By 1720 New Orleans was not yet finished, but it
was already a town. And already it had a varied
population: hardy wood rangers from Canada who
had come to the territory to seek fur, Indian traders,
escaped slaves from the British colonies to the east of
Louisiana, and a few brave Frenchmen. The year
before, 147 black slaves had been brought to Louisiana from the West Indian island colony of Santo
Domingo (today Haiti) to help build New Orleans

and other towns in the territory. In the following
years, other shiploads of slaves would arrive from
both the West Indies and Africa.

It was a very lonely and frightening land for the
slaves, especially for those who had just been brought
from Africa. They had been taken by force from their
homeland, packed by the hundreds into the holds of
ships whose captains cared nothing for their comfort,
and carried thousands of miles to a strange land to be
worked and whipped and treated like animals. And
what was worse, they could not understand either
their masters or one another; they were from many

different tribes and spoke many different languages. The slave traders, loading their ships on the Gold Coast of Africa, were careful to choose blacks from different tribes in order that they would not be able to talk to one another and plan an escape. When the ships arrived in the West Indies and America the white planters did the same thing, for the same reason: if the slaves could not talk to one another, then they could not plan an escape or a revolt against their masters. Gradually, the slaves learned the language of their masters and learned to adapt as best they could to the new country in which they found themselves.

Although no type of slavery can be called bearable, the slaves in early Louisiana generally enjoyed better circumstances than those in many other parts of the New World. Louisiana was a very young colony, and there was not yet the strong class system of an established society. There were no huge plantations or industries requiring the work of many laborers. Some slaves were imported to be servants for the leaders of the colony, but probably the majority of the first slaves were brought in to help build the city that was to become its capital.

CHAPTER 2

New Orleans Is Built

The building of New Orleans was begun in 1718, sponsored by the French court but directed by a Scotsman named John Law. By that time, the French court had lost interest in the territory of Louisiana and had put aside plans to build it up or to find settlers to populate it. Law, on the other hand, was most interested in the possibilities for profit in colonizing the territory. In 1717, Law founded the Compagnie de l'Occident (Company of the West) and applied for a charter that would enable him to oversee the colony for the French crown. King Louis XIV had died, and as King Louis XV was only five years old, the regent, Philippe, Duc d'Orléans, ruled for him. Philippe quickly granted the requested charter, happy to place the responsibility for the bothersome colony in the hands of someone else. Although Law would direct the colony, its governors would be French. Law immediately set about constructing a city in the fertile crescent that Iberville had so admired.

By 1721, New Orleans had reached that stage in its building at which it could be called a real town. Early in that year the French surveyor Adrien de Pauger began to lay out the section that is now called the Old City, with narrow streets and L-shaped houses set right up against the walkways on either side of the street. In November of the same year the first census was taken: it showed that there were 145 men, 65 women, 38 children, 29 white servants, 172 black slaves, and 21 Indian slaves. The whole population was only 470, so it was not a very large town; but in 1722 the French governor used his influence to have it declared the capital of Louisiana. He was Pierre Le Moyne's brother, Jean-Baptiste Le Moyne, better known as Sieur de Bienville—and he, like his brother, considered the site of New Orleans the most beautiful section along the Mississippi.

Of course, now that New Orleans was the capital, it was even more important that the city become a respectable place. The majority of the men were soldiers, trappers, indentured servants bound to service for three years, miners, and galley slaves—and they did not care much about being responsible citizens. Almost all the women were former inmates of French prisons who had been forced to come to the New World; the rest were Choctaw squaws and African slave women. Something, it was felt, had to be done to bring in a better class of citizens.

The Compagnie de l'Occident and the French government began to encourage further colonization of Louisiana. John Law sent representatives throughout France and into Germany to find new settlers. In glowing terms they described the rich land and wonderful opportunities in Louisiana and offered the hard-working peasants a fresh start, promising land, seed, and livestock. Before long the colony saw a great many new settlers.

As part of their plan toward order, the French early took care that laws were drawn up to regulate relations between the whites and the blacks in the colony. By March 1724, the government in France had formulated a series of laws called the Code Noir (Black Code). Although some of the laws were meant to regulate the conduct of blacks, such as those forbidding blacks and whites to marry each other, others were designed to protect them. The last law especially did so:

> We grant to manumitted [freed] slaves the same rights, privileges and immunities which are enjoyed by free-born persons. It is our pleasure that this merit in having acquired their freedom shall produce in their favor, not only with regard to their persons, but also to their property, the same effects which our other subjects derive from the happy circumstances of their having been born free.[2]

Slavery in Louisiana was not at this time the harsh, brutal institution that it was in many other American colonies. Although many German, Scottish, and French farmers were settling along the Mississippi upriver from New Orleans, they were small farmers. Most could not afford slaves, and those who could afford a few often worked side by side with them. The Black Code required white masters to feed and clothe and house their slaves adequately, even when illness or old age prevented them from working. Slaves were not to be worked on Sundays and Holy Days, and would be taken away from their masters if they were. Of course, these laws were not obeyed by everyone; but generally the slaves were better treated than in other colonies.

The growing town of New Orleans required more and more skilled laborers—carpenters, bricklayers, tilers—as well as more and more servants. The majority of slaves worked in these types of occupations. As early as 1722, there were free blacks in New Orleans and the area surrounding it. Like everyone else in the colony, slaves and free people of color were required to be of the Catholic faith, and baptisms, marriages, and burials of colored people were recorded in the church registers. Many of these documents are still in St. Louis Cathedral, including the one of the twenty-third marriage held in the cathedral in 1724. That was the marriage of a free colored couple.

But while laws such as these were obeyed, many others were broken. The law broken most often was that which made illegal any unions between blacks and whites. Such unions had occurred almost from the beginning, mostly because there were very few white women in the new colony. It was a commonly accepted practice for white masters to take slaves as their mistresses. The masters chose the best-looking slave women; as the years wore on and more French blood entered the veins of the African slaves, the whites then preferred the lighter slave women.

In the 1750s France and Spain were engaged in a war against Prussia that also involved other European nations. The war lasted seven years; it was not until November 1763 that a formal peace treaty was signed. That treaty might have been signed earlier if either of the two countries had wanted Louisiana.

Louis XV, who by now was old enough to rule in his own right, had been convinced by his ministers that Louisiana meant more trouble than profit to France. Despite attempts to bring order to the colony, lawlessness and high living prevailed among the people, who were still mostly men. The attempts at bringing other colonists into Louisiana had not measured up to France's expectations. Also, the population was not growing at the rate a young, progressing colony needed, and so far the area had not proved a source of wealth for France.

After the treaty of 1763 was signed and the long

Seven Years' War was ended, it seemed to all
concerned in France that the best thing to do would
be to make a gift of Louisiana to Louis's cousin,
Charles III of Spain. That way, the colony would be
off their minds but safely in the hands of an
ally—there would be no danger of its falling to the
English. Charles III of Spain, however, did not want
Louisiana either. Spain's holdings in the New World
were extensive, and were difficult enough to control
from afar without being increased by the addition of
Louisiana. Charles refused. Louis XV persisted.
France was determined to give up the colony, and
finally Spain accepted the donation.

When the announcement of Spain's acceptance
of the colony was made two years later, the French in
Louisiana were furious. They were Frenchmen, they
insisted, and would not be ruled by Spaniards.
Resistance was so strong that Spanish rule was not
firmly established in the colony until 1769, after the
Spanish appealed to the French for help in bringing
about order. In that year, an Irishman by the name of
O'Reilly—eventually almost everyone called him
"Bloody O'Reilly"—arrived with three thousand
Spanish troops. It didn't take long for Bloody
O'Reilly to put things back in order! After that,
although the people of Louisiana did not like it, they
began to accept Spanish rule; but they never became
Spanish. Although Spanish was the official language

of the courts and other chief public offices, French continued to be spoken everywhere else. At dances and other social activities the native Louisianians ignored the Spanish, and sometimes there were fights and duels. Some of the Spanish officials managed to win esteem—Governor Don Bernardo de Gálvez was very popular—but of course a mostly French population could never be truly happy under Spanish rule.

The Spanish tried hard to increase the population of the colony. In 1785, they imported from France more than 1,600 Acadians. These people were originally from Nova Scotia, but they had been forced from their homeland by the English thirty years before. Although most had fled to other British provinces in America, some had found refuge in France. It was these people who were persuaded to settle in the new territory, where they became known as Cajuns. Like other groups before them, they intermarried with the French and Germans, with the small group of settlers from the thirteen British colonies to the east, with the slaves, and with the growing class of free blacks.

Under the Spanish, marriage among the various groups in Louisiana took place more often than under the French. Three Spanish governors of Louisiana married into important French families in New Orleans. One Spanish governor, Don Antonio de Ulloa, even gave his permission for a Frenchman to marry a Negro woman. After a while, although most Louisianians continued to marry within their own group, the number of persons of mixed heritage grew. This, combined with the fact that the Spanish freed many blacks while they ruled in Louisiana, caused a sudden growth in the number of free people of color. While in 1769 the census listed 99 free people of color, in 1789 the number was 1,147.

Spanish rule was favorable to free men and women of color. It was the custom that any Frenchman or Spaniard who fathered a child by a Negro woman should free that child. Many adult slaves as well were freed under the Spanish. It was also under the Spanish that free people of color began to be regarded as a separate class between the whites and the slaves—and closer, in rights and status, to the whites. The *gens de couleur,* as they were called, enjoyed their separate status, and took many steps to keep their distance from both the whites and the slaves. After a time, they would not associate with the slaves or even with newly freed blacks. After all, they told themselves, these slaves and dark freedmen had no education and no manners. The *gens de couleur* did not like the whites very much either, although they imitated white customs and manners. White newcomers who were not French or Spanish were snubbed almost as much as the slaves were.

The free men of color followed many trades,

among them ironworking. They made most of the lacy iron balconies that can still be seen in the Old City. It was under the Spanish that the oldest section of New Orleans was built to look much as it does today, for the great fires of 1788 and 1794 had destroyed most of the wooden buildings constructed by the French. The Spanish were in power when the colony began to erect public buildings, and thus many of these structures, especially churches, are Spanish in style. The tiled roofs and the little patios, shaded by banana or palm trees and tropical plants, are Spanish. Free men of color helped erect these buildings; they were the best stonemasons. They also became tailors. They saved their money and bought property.

The free women of color had many occupations, too. Most of them worked in the homes of whites as cooks or maids. Some earned their living as hairdressers or *modistes,* dressmakers. In those days, there were no beauty salons; hairdressers went to the homes of their customers to style their hair. A skilled hairdresser could make an excellent living. Clothing was all handmade. Although a few dressmakers had shops, where their clients came to look at patterns and select fabrics or to be fitted for their gowns, many also worked out of their own homes, going to the homes of their customers to do fittings. A *modiste* who could re-create with skill the fashions in the style

books from Paris also made an excellent living. Other free women of color were *marchandes,* selling *cala* or flowers.

The most beautiful light-skinned women usually became the mistresses of white men, and they made a good living, too. Some had fine dresses of silk and taffeta, ostrich plumes and jewels in their hair, necklaces and bracelets and earrings and rings. Some even had their own carriages with matched horses. They lived in fine houses—the best known of which were located on Rampart Street—provided by their white men friends. But many lived quietly as second wives to their white men, keeping second homes for them, taking care of the children they had together. The children were often taken by their father to be recorded in the St. Louis Cathedral register as his natural children—a record that would later be prized by those children as evidence of their white parentage. It was just as if the man had two families, and the free woman of color was content to have a white husband for half the time. Most of the rich Frenchmen had free women of color for mistresses, and many of the Spanish officers and civilians did, too. Such a relationship was called a *plaçage.* In the days when there were more white men than white women, it was a very common and accepted practice. A favorite saying in the colored community at the time was, *"Un bon plaçage vaut mieux qu'un mauvais mariage"* ("A good *plaçage* is better than a bad marriage").

The *plaçage* was certainly better than no marriage at all. Although the women sometimes worried that the *plaçage* was not a marriage in the eyes of the Church, the advantages outweighed the disadvantages. The advantages were those of a blood union with a white family: having children lighter than oneself, and gaining higher social status and greater educational and economic opportunities. Gradually, as more Europeans came to Louisiana and the number of white women grew, the practice began to be criticized; but it continued on up until the Civil War.

As more and more European women arrived, however, at least some governmental attempt to prevent *plaçages* was necessary, and in 1786 the Spanish governor Estéban Miro took steps to satisfy the European women. On June 2 he ordered that free women of color who earned their living as the mistresses of white men were to give up the practice and look for other ways to support themselves; otherwise, they would be expelled from the colony. Miro's decree further ordered that free women of color were no longer to wear too many jewels or to deck their hair with plumes, and that from then on they would be required to tie up their hair in a

tignon—a kerchief used as a headdress—as a symbol of their lower status.

Governor Miro's decree was not really obeyed. White men and free women of color continued their relationships, only not so openly. And many free women of color turned their *tignons* into a further asset to their beauty, making them of fine silks and decking them with jewels.

These unions between white men and free

women of color were not the only unlawful thing that
went on in New Orleans. Gambling was rampant,
whether at the table, or at cockfights, or at the endless
domino games. And if laziness could be called
unlawful, then New Orleans was the most crime-
ridden city in the world. The people, white and
colored, do not seem to have had much ambition.
There were few schools, and many people could
barely read or write. Very few were professionals, and
there were no banks or libraries. It was not until the
1790s that the first theater was built and the first
newspaper was begun. People did their jobs and
enjoyed a close and active family life, but they spent
most of their time and energy having fun—gambling,
attending balls and dances, celebrating religious holidays. This was as true of the free people of color as of
the whites. Hard work was meant for slaves.

The citizens of New Orleans wanted prosperity
as much as anyone else, but they preferred to seek it
by buying up paper money, which was not worth very
much, and hoping it would rise in value. They had
only one real source of wealth: they owned much
property, and they made money by selling and
renting lots and houses. That was fine for them then;
but great changes were in store for Louisiana, and
neither the white nor the colored population would be
ready for them.

CHAPTER 3

The United States
Buys Louisiana

By the end of the 1790s, France had changed its mind about Louisiana. The young first consul, Napoleon Bonaparte, saw New Orleans' promise as a port, and Louisiana's promise as the basis for a colonial empire. He began to negotiate with Spain to regain the same territory his country had so eagerly given up just a few decades before. By the spring of 1801, the news came—Spain had ceded Louisiana back to France!

The large majority of Louisianians rejoiced. The Spanish occupation had never really been accepted. Although the Spanish language was required in the courts and important public offices, the people's everyday speech had remained French. In other areas of life as well French culture prevailed. But the French never retook control of Louisiana; despite the treaty Spain ran the colony until the end of 1803. After that, to the great dismay of the inhabitants, yet another country took control.

Although Louisiana had hardly been touched by them, important and shattering events had been happening in the British colonies to the east. A war of independence had begun in 1775 and a new nation, the United States, had been born. This new nation, although it was independent, was not very strong militarily, and when its president, Thomas Jefferson, heard that Spain had ceded Louisiana back to the French, he knew he must take action. Jefferson was bothered by the ambition of Napoleon Bonaparte, who quite clearly had ideas of empire on his mind. There was a real and frightening possibility that Napoleon's troops would someday arrive at the Mississippi and grab the vast potential empire beyond its western banks. Immediately, Jefferson wrote to United States Minister Robert R. Livingston in France to seek a price on the Floridas (the Spanish-held territories east of Louisiana) and on New Orleans. He did not care about the rest of the territory of Louisiana.

Livingston began negotiations with Charles Maurice de Talleyrand, Napoleon's representative; and by the time James Monroe, sent by Jefferson as minister extraordinary to France on the matter, arrived, an agreement had almost been reached.

While many of Napoleon's advisors urged that France retain control of Louisiana, Napoleon did not feel that France's small naval force could hold the territory, now that a revolt in the French colony of Santo Domingo was occupying most of the French army and war with England loomed on the horizon. Before Monroe reached France, Napoleon directed his representatives to begin negotiations with Livingston and to offer the United States the opportunity to purchase, not just the Floridas and New Orleans, but the whole of Louisiana as well. After Monroe arrived, it took just two weeks for France and the United States to conclude the greatest real estate bargain in history: altogether, 80 million francs ($15 million) for a territory from which fifteen states or parts of states would be formed.

In many ways, New Orleans was the key to the future strength and power of the young country, for the United States would have been much smaller and much weaker without it. Napoleon knew that giving up Louisiana to Jefferson would mean just that. Speaking of the treaty, Napoleon said, "This accession of territory strengthens forever the power of the United States; and I have just given to England a maritime rival, that will sooner or later humble her pride." [3]

But while the Louisiana Purchase marked the beginning of America's influence, it marked the beginning of the end of the French influence.

When the United States took charge in Louisiana, it was like occupying a foreign country. Mostly

French-speaking, predominantly Catholic, Louisianians strongly resented their new American—and
chiefly Protestant—rulers, who seemed in many ways
everything that they themselves were not. New Orleans became truly divided into two communities:
those inhabitants of French culture, who had come
before 1803, and those Americans who came after,
although the latter group would quite quickly begin
to outnumber the former. Not only was the French
culture threatened; even more, the economic liveli-
hood of French-speaking Louisianians was in danger.
Thousands of Americans flocked to Louisiana. Some
were loud and brawling backwoodsmen and boat-
men—but although they were viewed with great
distaste by the natives, they were not a serious threat.
The real danger came from the young, ambitious
Americans who saw unlimited opportunities for
wealth and power and prestige in the new territory:
young lawyers eager for the many administrative jobs
opening up, and aware of the demand for legal talent;
merchants anxious to gain a piece of the booming
commerce of the port of New Orleans; planters
looking for cheap, rich land; doctors; apprentices.
Wave upon wave poured into Louisiana and especially into New Orleans, and the French culture
seemed in danger of being swept away by the tide.

The free people of color in Louisiana were

affected just as much as the whites—and in some ways more. In the space of just twenty years, from 1790 to 1810, lightning-fast changes took place in the free colored community, and in the black community as a whole.

Two of these changes concerned inventions: a sugar-granulating process and the cotton gin. For many years, Louisiana planters had been looking for a dependable staple crop. They had tried raising silkworms for silk, but that had not worked. For a time indigo, a bad-smelling plant that produced a fine blue dye, seemed the answer; but in the 1790s that endeavor, too, was just about given up. Sugarcane had long been grown for syrup and for alcoholic drinks, but no process had been developed to make the sugar crystallize. Then, in 1791, a Spanish magistrate named Mendez was successful in his experiments to crystallize sugar, and a chain of events began that would eventually make Louisiana the main sugar-growing state.

The cotton gin made cotton another important Louisiana industry, one that would later outrank sugar in importance. Before the invention of the cotton gin, workers had separated the lint from the cotton seeds by hand, and then packed the small pieces of lint into bales; it had been slow and arduous work. The cotton gin made both processes easy and fast. The machine's teeth caught the lint and pulled it from the cottonseeds; then a revolving brush on the same machine took the lint from the teeth. One machine could now do the jobs it had taken many workers to do. It could pack bales and bales of cotton in a single day.

Both of these inventions brought about an increase in the slave population of Louisiana. With expanded production now possible, more sugarcane and cotton fields could be planted and large harvests could be made. All of this required a plentiful supply of slave labor.

Another event affected the *free* colored population—the revolution in Santo Domingo. A revolt of the slaves against the white French planter class began there in 1791 and lasted for thirteen bloody years, until the rebels succeeded in founding the independent Negro Republic of Haiti in 1804. During these years, thousands of the French were massacred, but thousands more escaped. The free people of color in Santo Domingo, who, like their counterparts in Louisiana, had identified more with the whites than with the slaves, suffered the same fate: some were massacred, others escaped. They sought shelter on neighboring islands—Trinidad, Jamaica, Guadeloupe, Puerto Rico, and especially Cuba, across the Windward Passage; but when, in 1809, Napoleon invaded Spain, they were forced by Spanish Cuba to leave. Some ten thousand of these once-again-refugees found their way to New Orleans, swelling the population of the city. Like most refugees, they were greeted with suspicion and distrust. Where would they be housed? How would they live? Whose jobs would they take away? How would they change the culture of the city? They were distrusted as much by the native Louisianians as by the Americans—with the exception, perhaps, of the Creoles of color.

The refugees of color from Haiti built St. Augustine Church in the early 1840s, and soon after that three young women of color from Haiti founded the Order of the Holy Family for other young women of color who wished to become nuns. The refugees from Haiti brought with them useful trades, better education, and a culture that was older and more sophisticated. The free people of color among them had been free for several generations already—some families since the sixteenth century—and they were able to teach the New Orleans free people of color many things.

In numbers, the colored population was increased most by this influx. By 1810, the colored inhabitants had increased, from 1,500 in 1805, to 5,000, giving them a majority of 59 percent.

The small American white population became much more alarmed at this increase than were the French whites. The Americans were just beginning to exert their influence over the French population, and the last thing they needed was a whole new wave of French-speaking citizens. There was little they could do to prevent the immigration of white French, but they could take steps to limit the immigration of free colored people and slaves, for in that they would have the full backing of the federal government. In 1808 the United States had passed a law banning the foreign slave trade, and a Louisiana law barred the entrance of all free people of color into the territory. These laws were very much in line with the overall attitude of the Americans toward the colored people, be they free or slave, in Louisiana. This attitude particularly affected the free people of color.

At the time of the Louisiana Purchase the free people of color enjoyed many rights and immunities. Many were wealthy and educated, owning property and sometimes even slaves; in appearance, they were often indistinguishable from whites. In the treaty of cession signed by France and the United States, one article, reported to have been written by Napoleon himself, provided that

the inhabitants of the ceded territory shall be . . . admitted as soon as possible . . . to the enjoyment of all the rights, advantages, and immunities, of citizens of the United States; and in the meantime, they shall be maintained and protected in the free enjoyment of their liberty, and the religion which they profess.

Naturally, the free people of color expected the Americans to recognize these words as a statement of their rights as free persons. They were very disillusioned when the Territory of Orleans entered the Union as Louisiana, the eighteenth state, in 1812, and its constitution did not so much as mention Negroes or slavery or free people of color. Worse than that, by stating that the rights to vote, serve in the legislature, and bear arms were reserved for free white males, it clearly ignored the special privileges free people of color had enjoyed under the French and Spanish, and during the first nine years of American rule. In fact, they would have no political rights at all—not even the right of citizenship. They had to put the initials "f.m.c." or "f.w.c." (free man of color, free woman of color) after their names whenever they wrote them; and these initials could not even be capital letters! They would be hardly better than slaves, and they resented the change deeply.

It was at this time that the Louisiana-born free people of color began calling themselves Creoles, and insisting that others call them that, too. Now that being a free person of color didn't make one any different from an American Negro freedman, or for that matter (now that the new laws had been passed) from a slave, they wanted to be called something that would separate them from these other groups.

Even though with the new laws the Creoles had lost many privileges, their lives did not change overnight. The change came gradually. For example, they still bore arms. When the Spanish were in power a free colored militia had been set up, and, while the Americans wanted to disband this militia, they were afraid of what might happen if they tried to take away the guns of its 300 men. In the end they allowed the militia to continue.

Later, they would be glad they had: the soldiers fought bravely against the British in the Battle of New Orleans in 1815. They were joined by a group of

the Haitian refugees. Savary, a free man of color from the island, organized 150 of the immigrants; he was later praised for his bravery.

When the war was over, General Andrew Jackson made a speech about the valor of his soldiers of color.

Soldiers! From the shores of Mobile I collected you to arms; I invited you to share in the perils and to divide the glory of your white countrymen. I expected much from you, for I was not uninformed of those qualities which must render you so formidable to an invading foe. I knew that you would endure hunger and thirst and all the hardships of war. I knew that you loved the

land of your nativity, and that, like ourselves, you had to defend all that is most dear to man; but you surpass my hopes. I have found in you, united to those qualities, that noble enthusiasm which implies to great deeds.

Soldiers! The President of the United States shall be informed of your conduct on the present occasion, and the voice of the Representatives of the American Nation shall applaud your valor, as your general now praises your ardor. The enemy is near; his sails cover the lakes; but the brave are united; and if he finds us contending among ourselves, it will be for the prize of valor, and fame its noblest reward.[4]

Actually, free men of color saw military service as early as 1729, when they fought, together with black slaves, under Governor Etienne Périer against the Natchez Indians. They fought so well that Governor Périer reported: "If the blacks did not cost so much, and if their labors were not so necessary to the colony, it would be better to turn them into soldiers and to dismiss those we have, who are so bad and so cowardly." [5] They also fought under Governor Bienville against the Chickasaws in the early 1730s; under Spanish Governor Gálvez against the British in 1779; and in many other battles.

CHAPTER 4

The Golden Age for Creoles of Color

After the Battle of New Orleans and the end of the War of 1812, the city grew as never before. More and more people from Ireland and Germany came in, as well as white Americans and American Negro freedmen. Slaves were brought in, too, to work on the big plantations. The Americans were buying up land and starting large farms, and in the city they were opening banks and businesses. A great deal of money was being attracted, but not very much of it was going into the pockets of the earlier settlers. The French inhabitants of New Orleans did not have the business sense that the Americans had. They looked down their noses at the Americans and tried not to have much to do with them. They would not even learn English.

The Creoles did pretty much the same. Many of the immigrants from Europe challenged them in the trades that were their main source of living. The chief occupations of the better class of free colored laborers included mechanics, cabinetmaking, shoemaking, cigarmaking, tailoring, construction, and hunting to supply the city with meat. The newcomers, who were unskilled, found it hard to move into these jobs. They were much more successful in taking away the jobs of the poorer colored classes—draymen, cabmen, and servants in the hotels. By the middle of the century, hardly a colored face could be seen in these jobs. As the number of Negro freedmen grew, it was sometimes hard for the Creoles not to be mistaken for them. To guard against this, the Creoles refused to learn English, and held themselves aloof from white Americans and Negro freedmen alike. The Creole community drew into itself, which was foolish in a way. The Creoles would have done better to watch and learn from the Americans. But this self-isolation was also fortunate, because it caused a renaissance in the Creole culture.

Many of the wealthier Creoles were musicians, merchants, money and real estate brokers. A few had been educated in France, and now it became very important that their own children be educated there. The majority of wealthy Creoles, however, like most of the wealthy white Louisianians of French culture, had to be content with hiring tutors to teach their children French history, and proper French grammar—to guard against the American words that were making their way into New Orleans French speech—

and music and literature. The theater was very important, too, and in the evening they would go to the Théâtre d'Orléans at Orleans and Bourbon streets. The theater had separate sections for whites, for free people of color, and for slaves, and the silks and jewels and feathers on the Creole women were just as fine as those of the whites. The Creole women took great care with their *tignons.* They had found myriad ways to wrap them about their heads, and by decorating the silk with pearls and colored stones, they could create exquisite turbans.

The most legendary aspect of this golden era for the Creoles was the quadroon ball. Few writers on this period of Louisiana history have neglected to mention these balls, although in the process and over time they became highly romanticized. According to legend, they were glamorous affairs, held in the Orleans Ballroom, next to the Théâtre d'Orléans, or at the St. Philip Street Theatre or the Washington Ballroom. Beautiful young Creole girls, escorted by their mothers, would attend these balls, hoping to meet a young Frenchman with whom they could form a *plaçage.* The balls were attended also, according to legend, by *courtisanes,* beautiful women who did not seek a "husband" but a number of admiring men who would provide them with dresses and jewelry in exchange for their favors.

While undoubtedly there were social functions of

some kind in which Creole women and Frenchmen met, it is unlikely that they were very glamorous or that those who attended them, white and Creole alike, were very respectable. The majority of young Creole women desired a quiet and virtuous life with a home and children.

What about the Creole men? There were no balls held in order for them to meet Frenchwomen. One wonders if they did not resent the social customs that allowed their women to associate so openly with Frenchmen; that allowed Frenchmen access to their women, and Creole women to invite the favors of Frenchmen. Yet if there was resentment, it was not shown publicly. At the Théâtre d'Orléans, in the section reserved for free persons of color, the Creole men attended their women with the greatest gallantry, appearing not to notice the attention being paid the women by the men in the white section. Of course not all Creole women entered into *plaçage* arrangements with Frenchmen; many married Creole men.

A number of Creole families amassed considerable wealth. The 1830 census showed that an aggregate of more than 750 Creole families owned, among them, almost 2,500 slaves. Most of these Creoles had achieved their prosperity through investment in real estate, but a few became rich in other ways. One, Norbert Rillieux, made his fortune—and, in a sense, a fortune for Louisiana as well—through the invention of a more effective sugar-refining process. Rillieux was born into an upper-class New Orleans Creole family early in the 1800s, and was fortunate enough to be sent to France for his education. While attending school in France, he became immersed in scientific studies, and by the age of twenty-four he was publishing technical findings and winning praise from French scientists. He would have liked to return to Louisiana to pursue a scientific career at home, but he knew that he would not have in Louisiana many of the opportunities he enjoyed in France.

Influential whites in Louisiana learned of Rillieux's work and decided the young scientist should come home. Some of his experiments had been in the field of sugar engineering, and Theodore Packwood, a planter, offered him a well-paying job to continue these experiments for his plantation.

It will be remembered that in 1791 a Spanish magistrate named Mendez had developed a process to make sugar crystallize; but the process had not been suitable for mass production. Rillieux worked for several years, conducting experiment after experiment, trying to find a method for evaporating the liquid from the sugarcane to leave only the fine, dry sugar so much in demand throughout the country. Finally he found it—the "multiple effect" process of evaporation—and in 1843 he received a patent for it.

His process laid the foundation for all modern industrial evaporation.

By the middle 1840s, it became noticeable that something had happened to the Creoles: their numbers were greatly reduced. In the Creole community, rumors abounded about Creoles going north, going west. It had been getting harder and harder for them to live in Louisiana. In 1830, a law had been passed prohibiting the writing or publishing of anything that might breed discontent among the slaves, as well as the teaching of any slaves. In 1845 came another law forbidding the lodging, entertainment, or employment of any free people of color not born in Louisiana; the next year this law was made stronger. About the same time, a law was passed barring free people of color from the public schools—even though they still had to pay taxes for the support of the schools. Colored families had to find tutors and other means of schooling for their children until 1848. Then, Madame Couvent, a wealthy black woman born in Guinea, opened a school for all free people of color, charging tuition only to those who could pay it. By the time of the Civil War there were fifteen or twenty small private schools for people of color, some of them admitting only wealthy, light-skinned Creoles.

The Creoles, despite the fact that they considered themselves separate from other free people of

color, suffered from this general anti-colored feeling in the late 1830s and 1840s. By that time the Americans were firmly settled in Louisiana, and their legal attitude toward black people, slave and free, was much more harsh than that of the French or the Spanish. Many Creoles could not continue to live under a government that did not consider them any different from other colored people. It was easier to leave, and many did so.

Among those Creoles who stayed, the determination not to blend in with the rest of the colored freedmen grew. In fact, this threat to their identity seemed to spark a new creativity, a new awareness of their unique status. In 1843, the first magazine to contain writings by Creoles, *L'Album Littéraire (The Literary Album)*, was issued; it was a collection of poems and short stories. Everyone in the Creole community bought the magazine, and many read it so often that they came to know the poems and stories by heart. Today it is hard for whites and even young blacks to imagine how much that magazine meant to the Creoles, who had never before seen anything published by people of their own kind. The feeling can best be compared to that of American blacks in the 1960s when, for the first time, blacks began to appear in television and magazine advertising. Two more issues of the magazine came out before J. L. Marciacq, the Frenchman who had published it, ran out of money and could not afford to print any more. He was a brave man, nevertheless. No white man was expected to help the Creoles in such a way, but Marciacq had tutored the children of many of the rich families of color and had come to understand the Creoles' desire to be recognized authors.

One such writer went on after Marciacq ended his enterprise. His name was Armand Lanusse; born in New Orleans in 1812, he had been educated in Paris. Some of his short stories and poems appeared in the three issues of *L'Album Littéraire,* and the fact that such a magazine had existed caused him to feel that it was possible to publish other writings by the Creoles—perhaps a collection of poems. Two or three years after the advent of *L'Album Littéraire,* Lanusse published a collection of eighty-seven poems by Creoles. He chose as its title *Les Cenelles* (*Holly Berries*). The holly, native to Louisiana, does not grow quickly. The Creoles, too, were natives of Louisiana and, in Lanusse's opinion, had taken a long time to "grow" in terms of literary output. However, he did not mention anywhere in the book that its authors were Creole.

CHAPTER 5

The War and What Came After

By the late 1850s, the Creole community had turned its interest from the literary achievements of some of its members to events that were taking place in the larger society. Even at that time there was much talk of the South seceding from the Union. New Orleans newspapers discussed the possibility in their editorial columns, and more and more—on the street corners, in public places, and in private homes —the talk was of the apparently unsolvable differences between the North and the South.

Slavery was only one of the questions over which North and South disagreed. There were other antagonisms. The North was becoming more industrialized; the South was still chiefly agricultural. The industrial North, being more wealthy, was trying to impose its desires upon the South. The South, on the other hand, which supplied the North with many raw materials, was trying to use this leverage to impose its desires upon the North. Although southerners at first felt that if they took a strong stand on the questions that divided them from the North, the North would give in, by the early 1860s the only solution seemed to lie in war. The South seceded from the Union, and the Civil War was on.

The Creoles of color had mixed feelings about the war. Their status as a class had become worse during the years leading up to the war. Just before its outbreak, the government of Haiti sent representatives to the United States to recruit people to move to Haiti; they concentrated especially upon New Orleans, for it was here that so many of the Haitian refugees from the trouble of 1804 had settled. Some wealthy Creoles put up money to help those who wanted to go to Haiti, and several hundred did go at that time. They were looking for a better life in a place where they were recognized as a special group and not just as people of color. It is not known how many Creoles eventually went to Haiti, but it was probably a substantial number.

When the war broke out, the Creoles became very much divided—which should not seem strange, because they were right in the middle. If the South won, they would perhaps be able to hold on to their status as a separate class between the slaves and the whites. If the North won, and freed the slaves, they would be in danger of being treated like all other free people of color; but at the same time there was the hope that all people, white and colored, would be treated the same. In the early days of the war many Creoles favored the South, and 1,500 of them offered their services to the Confederacy in 1861. Their help was accepted, and they were organized into a regiment to defend the city. Others gave money to the Confederate cause. But when, in 1862, New Orleans fell to the Union troops, many of the Creole soldiers went over to the Union cause. Some Creoles continued to support the Confederacy, but a great number now were on the side of the North.

Why did so many Creoles gravitate to the northerners, whose manners and customs they disdained? Chiefly, because the South drove them to do so. In 1855, for example, a law had been passed requiring free people of color to have a permit if they wished to move about the streets. As war drew closer, more and more restrictions were placed upon them. They loved the South, but the South seemed bent upon destroying them. In addition the North offered many attractive promises to the Creoles. Although Lincoln's Emancipation Proclamation and the war resulted in freedom for the slaves and endangered the Creoles' separate status, the unshackling of such large numbers of illiterate black people meant the possibility that the Creoles could become powerful leaders of the black race. With this power, they could advance their own wealth and their own political position.

Everyone knows that there is power in numbers. As a result of the Emancipation Proclamation, the number of Negroes in New Orleans swelled quickly. Thousands of freedmen poured into the city because it was occupied by Union troops—the representatives of the government that had freed them. Between 1860 and 1870 the Negro population of New Orleans doubled, reaching 50,000. These people needed leadership, and many Creoles in the city were more than ready to take advantage of that need.

The Union victory and the end of the war ushered in a period of great influence on the part of the Creoles. It would have been even greater if men from other parts of the country had not seen the opportunity for influence also. With nearly all the white Louisianians deprived of power because of their part in the war, positions of leadership in politics were there for the asking, and were soon snatched up by men from many regions. In 1863 a group of Creoles called upon the governor to allow them the right of suffrage; they published their appeal in the newspapers and raised such a clamor that President Lincoln had to change his mind about not giving free people of color the vote. He decided that those free men of color who were intelligent and who had fought on the Union side should vote. This was fine news for the Creoles, who did not really want the newly freed slaves to get the vote and thus be on the same level as they; but of course in the end free men and freedmen alike were enfranchised. Negroes voted for the first time in Louisiana in 1865, and by 1868 the offices of lieutenant governor and state treasurer as well as other high positions were held by Creoles. Four Creoles and one freedman helped to found the Republican Party in Louisiana, and in the election of 1868 Major Francis Dumas, an octoroon (or one-eighth-Negro) born in France, lost the Republican nomination for governor by only two votes. André Monnette, J. H. Ingraham, A. E. Barbour, and four other Creoles served as state senators, and eight Creoles were state representatives, during the period 1868–1888.

Other Creoles, too, who did not wish to wield power through political office, held significant positions. Dr. Louis C. Roudanez, a Haitian refugee, edited and published the New Orleans *Tribune*; it was considered a very radical newspaper—much more so than any publication Armand Lanusse could ever have thought of editing. The homes of many wealthy Creoles—those of Arnold Bertonneau, Laurent Auguste, Formidor Desmazilières—became meeting places for Republicans, black and white. Creoles were invited to lavish drawing rooms to discuss political events and to offer their advice to ambitious Negroes. White men from the North, called carpetbaggers, attended these afternoon drawing-room sessions also, and listened with respect to the Creoles' advice, sipping toddies and bourbons. Even in the summer, when yellow fever often raged through the city, no one left for the country; no one wanted to miss anything.

Never before had there been so many opportunities for people of color. Between 1865 and 1880, New Orleans University, Straight University, Leland College, and Southern University were all founded in New Orleans. Medard Nelson also opened his school at this time. The other schools were mostly founded by missionary groups; but Monsieur Nelson, a dark Creole educated in France who spoke several languages, conducted his classes single-handed. Many whites attended the school, even at the beginning.

It was such a short time of ascendancy for the Creoles, but it was exhilarating.

It was, however, a very unsettled time as well. Federal troops patrolled the streets, guarding against outbreaks of fighting between whites and Negroes. Many Louisiana whites could not stand the thought of people of color holding government positions and enjoying political power. The Knights of the White Camellia, the White League, and other secret groups were formed; they marched often through the streets, armed with guns, as a show of force and to frighten the Negroes. In return, important Republicans organized Negroes into marching clubs and "Loyal

Leagues." Hardly a summer night passed that one or another of these groups did not march through the streets, their torches casting shadows upon the sleeping houses.

Meanwhile, other power struggles were going on. Although some of the carpetbaggers were truly interested in equality for colored people, many wished only to use the Negroes for their own ends; if betraying the Negroes would result in more power for themselves, they would not hesitate to do so. The Creoles and other influential people of color knew this, and were always wary of the white Republicans. Many of the freed slaves were illiterate and easily misled, and the Creoles found themselves in the strange position of safeguarding the rights of a people they had previously despised. This was why they had faced the Union victory with mixed feelings—before the war there had been the whites, the Creoles, and the Negroes; now there were only whites and Negroes. It did not matter how wealthy or how educated the Creoles were—they were grouped together with all the other people of color.

As the 1870s dawned, New Orleans was almost in a state of siege. The Republican Party was now a mass of factions, and before long Louisiana was faced with two governments, each claiming to be legally elected. Reinforcements for the federal troops in the city were moved in to help keep order, but it became dangerous to be out on the streets alone at night. The whites who had supported the Confederacy, and who had thus lost the right to vote, had been reenfranchised and had regained much of their power. The federal government, indeed much of the rest of the country, was tired of the troublesome South. Peace was becoming more important than justice, and some Creoles foresaw that it would only be a matter of time before the federal troops were pulled out and the South would be left to solve its own problems. Creoles knew very well what that would mean for them: the Negroes would be made to pay for their brief enjoyment of equality, and the Creoles, as people of color, would pay along with them. Their white carpetbagger friends, who had visited their salons and sipped their toddies and sought their advice, would not remain to help them. They would return to the North, leaving the Creoles to their fate.

In 1874 the Creoles were given a hint of what that fate could be. Five thousand Knights of the White Camellia staged a rebellion in the city, and the violence was even worse in the outlying parishes (or counties). Many blacks were killed—massacred, the Republican newspapers said. Most of the Creoles themselves escaped injury, partly because they hid inside their homes and partly because they still had some influence in the community. They realized, however, that if a mass demonstration of anti-black feeling were to break out, even they would not be safe from harm. This rebellion took place while Republicans still controlled the state government. The Creoles dreaded what would happen when the Democrats took control.

The year 1876 was a year both of Louisiana state elections and of a national presidential election, and there were many similarities between the two. Republicans had been in power for many years in both the White House and the Louisiana statehouse, but Democrats were now knocking on the doors. In Louisiana the acts of violence against people of color increased; but when Republicans complained, Democrats insisted the violence was in self-defense. Despite the Democrats' attempts to keep Negroes, especially, from the polls on Election Day, the results were so close that once again Louisiana was faced with two rival governments—this time, one Republican and one Democratic. The national elections were just as close; it was not until March, four months after the voting, that the presidency was decided. Rutherford B. Hayes, the Republican, was named winner over Samuel Tilden, the Democrat.

As far as the South was concerned, Tilden might just as well have won. Many of the Creoles believed that Hayes's victory was the result of a compromise: that in return for the presidency, the Republicans promised to pull the troops out of the South. Soon after Hayes's inauguration, the Democratic slate in Louisiana was declared the true government, and the federal troops were recalled.

In the outlying parishes—in Bayou Sara, in East Feliciana, and in others—there was an upsurge in violent acts against colored people; but even in these parishes the reenslavement of Negroes did not occur at once. Black people, in Louisiana as well as in other southern states, held their hard-won rights too dear to give them up without a struggle. Then, too, even though it was tired of the South's troubles, the rest of the country's memories were still too fresh to allow the South to have its way immediately.

Many Negroes continued for some years to have hope. But most of the Creoles did not feel hope. Perhaps that was because of their unique status, at least in their own eyes. Although they still considered themselves a special class, they were now merely Negroes in the eyes of others. It was strange: until then, even one drop of white blood had been enough to guarantee special privileges; from then on, a single drop of black blood was enough to guarantee no privileges at all.

The new status was especially hard for those who were nearly white or whose children were nearly white. For example, in 1861 the public schools had been opened for the first time to people of color—though many Creoles kept their children at home rather than send them to school with the children of freedmen. When segregation in the public school system was once again made official in 1877, the light-skinned Creoles who had enrolled their children in the public schools were forced to take them out.

Sometimes this was very embarrassing for the children. Once, an integrated school on Royal Street was visited by a White Leaguer. The man had a list of all the nonwhite girls, and as he called their names they had to stand, and then were forced to leave. The girls shrieked and sobbed, and when they were told

they could go to a colored public school, one replied, "Must I go to school with my own servants to escape an unmerited disdain?" Many Creole children would not go to the colored public schools, and those who did often refused to sit next to non-Creoles. Of course the non-Creoles did not like that at all. It was the beginning of a very bad time for everyone of color.

The change occurred gradually. A poll tax was instituted here, a railway segregation bill there, a "white primary election" somewhere else. Such anti-black measures came to be called "Jim Crow" laws; and after a time "Jim Crow" became, at least among blacks, in a way a person—a symbol of segregation and inequality. Jim Crow did not stride in; rather, he crept in. He crept in softly, but many of the Creoles saw him coming just the same. They met him in various ways.

A number of wealthy, prominent Creoles retained the hope that something could be done about these unjust laws. The South had lived under a system of equality of the races for a decade; these Creoles could not believe that responsible citizens would allow inequality to be reinstated. To fight the Jim Crow laws and to inspire other thinking individuals to fight them, too, a group of Creole men formed the Comité des Citoyens (Citizens' Committee) and established a newspaper, *The Crusader*, to fight the inferior status that was being forced upon them.

One of their first campaigns was waged against the law that required persons of color to ride in special streetcars and railway carriages. They took their case to the local courts and won their first suit against the separate-car law. However, their opponents then appealed to a higher court, and there the law was upheld. A man named Homère Plessy, a member of the Comité des Citoyens, decided to take the case all the way to the United States Supreme Court—but there, too, it was lost. The bitterly fought case, *Plessy v. Ferguson*, which the Court ruled upon in 1896, established for many years that the races could be separated as long as both enjoyed equal facilities and privileges. It was the famous "separate but equal" decision, and it opened the way for Jim Crow to march across the South. After that, segregation came quickly, in public places, in schools, in politics. There were separate facilities everywhere for whites and blacks, but these facilities were far from equal. In 1898, the last Negro official was removed from public office. By 1900, blacks in the South, although officially free, were little more than slaves again. The Comité des Citoyens, unable to combat Jim Crow, disbanded.

While prominent Creoles were attempting to fight the inferior status that was being imposed upon them, other, less wealthy and prominent Creoles went on very much as before. Many Creole women, for example, had long been house servants for white families, and they continued in this capacity after segregation was instituted. While when outside these white homes the Creole women may have found it harder to keep their dignity, inside they suffered no loss of status. Indeed, it is probable that they became even more formidable—for after all, the white families for whom they worked were partly to blame for the hard times that had come to the Creoles, if only because they had not tried to help them. The Creole servants played on this guilt. In 1880, Creole servant women were described in the following manner in a New Orleans newspaper:

> They are often intelligent, active, shrewd and capable. They generally perform whatever they undertake. They are too intelligent to be dishonest. They comprehend a look, an expression, as well as an order; they will fulfill a wish before it is expressed. They see everything, hear everything and say nothing. . . . They can tell a lie with the prettiest grace imaginable, or tell a truth in such a manner that it appears a lie. They read character with astonishing quickness, and once acquainted with the disposition of their employer will always anticipate his humors and make themselves pliable to his least wish. . . . Once initiated into the ways of the household, it is seldom necessary to give them an order. They know everything that is

required, and everything is done. If regularly paid and well treated, they will remain in a family for a generation. They demand a great deal of liberty when not actually employed, and will not remain in a house when they are not wholly free after working hours to go out or in as they please. They know everything that is going on, and a great deal more than they have any business to know.[6]

Actually, it was not very difficult to know a family's business, the way most houses in the Quarter were built. In the ordinary double cottages, all the rooms opened into one another, either with regular doors or with large folding or sliding doors. In addition, each room of each house opened into each room of its duplicate on either side. Even the attics of the houses opened into one another. The sounds in one house could be heard in the others—not only the servants but everyone else in the neighborhood knew one another's business. There were few secrets in the Old City. The Creole servant women made a point of knowing as much as they could. Their knowledge gave them what might be called "job security," for no master or mistress would dismiss a servant who knew too many secrets.

Some of the lighter-skinned Creoles had a third choice. Instead of trying to fight the new laws, instead of resigning themselves to life under them, they escaped. Some went to California, where they claimed Spanish blood; others went North and passed for white. Still others, it is said, remained right in New Orleans, blending into white society north of Canal Street.

They took a big chance, these Creoles who decided to pass for white. They knew that for the rest of their lives they would live in fear of discovery, especially if they had chosen to remain in New Orleans. There would always be the possibility that they might be recognized by whites they had known "before"; there would always be the possibility that some white might suspect their racial heritage and take steps to find out whether the suspicion was well founded. For the most part, the passing Creoles were helpless to forestall these possibilities. There was, however, one thing that could be done to help insure that their secret remained safe: they, or more often their families, could find and destroy the records in St. Louis Cathedral that were the only legal proof of their racial heritage.

It was ironic. Once, those birth records in St. Louis Cathedral had been prized by the Creoles—as the only legal proof that a child, born to a white man and a colored woman, was free-born. Later, they had served as proof of white French, and thus often aristocratic, blood. But for those Creoles who now chose to pass as white, they were the ominous key to the discovery of their real parentage. While once they

had been valued, in the closing years of the nineteenth century they were damned.

Those records in St. Louis Cathedral—how
much interest was shown in them during that period
after Jim Crow's arrival, when the Creole population
of New Orleans began to shrink so suddenly and
mysteriously! How often a particular volume was
requested, to be taken down from the shelves of the
dark, musty building adjacent to the cathedral,
dusted off, and opened by an official whose attention
had been brought to a case of passing—by a busy-
body who wished to confirm a suspicion, or by a
passing Creole who wished to remove the damning
evidence.

Literature on the Creoles of New Orleans is full
of stories involving these records. One writer, Edward
Larocque Tinker, recounted a story told him by an
old Creole woman. A dignified-looking middle-aged
man began to visit the registry building, asking for
the volumes of birth, marriage, and burial records
first for one year and then for another. He began with
the volume for the year 1815, and by the time the
records clerk had gotten out the years 1853 to 1860
for the man, the clerk had become quite fond of him.
But on that day, after the man had looked through
the volumes and then bade the clerk good-bye, the
clerk noticed that the volume for 1816 was out as
well. Leafing through the volume, he discovered a

page missing. Cursing under his breath, the clerk hurried out onto the street after the man.

"What do you mean by tampering with my archives!" he shouted at the man. "You're nothing but a fool like the rest of your race. You forgot about the index with all the facts in it." [7]

The man's face fell. The clerk would surely report the theft to the authorities, and all his efforts would have been in vain. In desperation, he showed the clerk a picture of his daughter. He had done it all for her, he insisted. She looked white, and the only proof that she had black blood lay in his own birth record, which listed his grandmother as an octoroon. The clerk explained he could not allow the page to remain missing, but he did relent—he did not report the theft to the authorities.

SECTION II
The Creole Today

CHAPTER 6

Creoles and the Color Line

Discriminatory laws piled upon one another for some years after 1900, each taking more civil and economic rights away from the Creoles of color as well as from non-Creole blacks. The Creoles could not accept being considered in the same class as other blacks; yet there was nothing they could do about it other than maintain their aloofness or continue to live below Canal Street. And so, many left New Orleans or passed into white society. Today there are no longer any wealthy Creoles of color in New Orleans. The Creoles who remained escaped also, in a way, by drawing into themselves—by throwing up a kind of protective wall against the outside society, and within that wall centering their lives around their community, their families, and their church. They went to great lengths to make sure their children married within the group and had little contact with non-Creoles.

For a while, they were almost forgotten by the

outside world; but then World War I broke out. Many blacks fought in World War I to "make the world safe for democracy," and when they returned they demanded democracy in their own country. Young Creole men of color went back to New Orleans dissatisfied to remain politically silenced. No great revolution resulted, but the seed of discontent was planted in the Creole community, and it slowly grew. It was echoed in the non-Creole Negro community, and gradually the younger Creoles began to identify themselves as American Negroes. World War II speeded up these changes.

Yet today the Creole of color is still a unique American, with his own special culture and life style. In fact, while the whites of French aristocratic descent have all but lost their culture, the Creoles have retained theirs intact in many ways. But now, with people of French and Spanish heritage, black and white, in New Orleans amounting to only about twenty or thirty thousand (or about 20 percent of the population), it seems that the days of the unique Creole culture are numbered.

The culture of the Creoles is still very French-influenced, although they have technically been American for over a century and a half. They still have a much greater class consciousness than most Americans. In America, although family background is important, one can enter the upper class or upper-middle class through wealth, occupation, or educational status. For the Creoles, what is all-important is family background; and next to that are wit, culture, manners, the role played by women, and the education of children. Family background has long set the Creole apart from the American Negro, who does not usually know his heritage. Many Creoles can trace back their family trees for several generations, and many family trees contain hardly a hint of slavery. Naturally, the Creoles are interested in others' family backgrounds and judge others on this basis. The same consciousness of class and family background is found, in some measure, among the white French descendants.

In the history of the Creoles, color has been almost as important as family background—not only skin color but hair texture and features. A surprising number of categories evolved to describe these traits and their various combinations. There were the octoroons (those having one eighth African blood), quadroons (one quarter African blood), mulattoes (one half African blood), and griffes (three quarters Negro, the offspring of a Negro and a mulatto) with some white characteristics but mostly Negro features. Then there were the marabon, somewhere between griffe and mulatto, with aquiline features, skin darker than quadroon but coppery, and soft, fine hair; and the briqué, with fairly light skin and reddish, woolly hair. In fact, hair texture seems to have been considered more important than skin color. In other words, a darker-skinned Creole with marabon hair could be more successful than a lighter-skinned Creole with woolly hair. Many Creole social clubs barred Creoles whose skin was too dark or whose hair was woolly; light-skinned Creole parishioners would ask their priest to demark certain sections for light-skinned, medium-dark, and dark-skinned people in the church. Darker-skinned Creole parents would seek a lighter-skinned match for their sons and daughters; lighter-skinned Creole parents would steer their children into matches within their own color range.

Today, the black pride and black consciousness movement has touched the Creoles of New Orleans, and the ideal skin color now is not almost-white but light-brown. Even many of those who still attach value to having a lighter skin are becoming slightly ashamed to admit it openly.

The Creoles have not been the only Negroes in America to feel this strong color consciousness. It is a natural outgrowth of the general color consciousness of Western society. The closer to white a person is, the "better" he is—the more opportunities he has, the more wealth he can acquire. Although all this is nonsense, color consciousness among the Creoles does exist, simply as an accommodation to the values of the predominant white society. Since those values still prevail—and strongly—some Creoles who are able to do so continue to pass into white society.

Sometimes this passing is accidental. Many a light-skinned Creole has found himself in the embarrassing situation of being taken for white in front of other Creoles, who know he is not white; or of being given a warning for speeding, when he knows he would be given a ticket if the traffic policeman realized he was a Creole. Sometimes a Creole will pass intentionally for just a short period, for a specific purpose. A Creole woman, for instance, might prefer the service at a white beauty parlor and thus pass as white in order to get her hair washed and set there. Some Creoles pass for a longer period of time, although still temporarily: a Creole might pretend he is white in order to get a better job. There are Creoles who work every day in the white world, passing as white for eight hours a day.

Permanent passing is not common among Creoles; except during periods of severe repression, such as after the Louisiana Purchase and after the Reconstruction era that followed the Civil War, it has generally been even less common than among non-Creole Negroes. The reason is obvious: total passing, for anyone, is a very difficult step, for it means leaving all that one has known, all one's family and friends and surroundings, and going to all that is unknown—into a completely different world. For the Creole, passing is a doubly difficult step: he is also leaving a basically French culture for an American one. Unless he travels to Canada or to one of the Canadian-French communities in the northern United States, he will have to change his culture twice over. Even so, passing is much more common than many whites believe.

Few in the New Orleans Creole community do not know of at least one Creole who has passed into white society. The reaction is mixed. There has always been understanding of why some Creoles pass—to escape discrimination, to have a greater chance—but in the twentieth century and with the rise of black consciousness, there has been a heightening of resentment toward this practice. Passing, after all, does mean a rejection of one's black heritage; and as many Creoles who pass do not better their status in any way except to be seen as white, they are resented by other Creoles for preferring roles as lower-class whites rather than upper-class Creoles. Despite this resentment, however, few Creoles would ever think of exposing fellow Creoles who are passing.

Thus, those Creoles who pass as white do not have much to fear from their fellow Creoles. Nor do they really have much to fear from New Orleans whites, who, living as they do in a very mixed urban culture, are more likely to see a person with a dark complexion as being of Latin ancestry. Outside New Orleans, however, there is much more danger of white suspicion and exposure.

In 1956, the Louisiana legislature passed a statute barring athletic contests between blacks and whites. In 1957, a New Orleans lightweight boxer named Ralph Dupas, who was scheduled to fight another white boxer, was accused of being nonwhite. It was charged that his last name was not Dupas but Duplessis, that he had been born not in New Orleans but in the parish of Plaquemines, and that his parents, Eveline and Peter Duplessis, were not white. The case was brought to the Louisiana State Athletic Commission and caused a furor in athletic circles; local and national press coverage was extensive. Although the commission ruled that no evidence had been presented to justify banning Ralph Dupas from the scheduled fight, anyone in Louisiana with the surname of Dupas or Duplessis would be suspect from then on. All such legal obstacles have since been repealed, but that does not mean citizen suspicions have abated.

Modern-day cases such as this, combined with the more recent tendency of light Creoles to identify with their black heritage, will probably lead to a decrease in the number of cases of passing. But the Creoles' relationship to other groups of people is not as important in their life style and culture as their individual relationships with one another—through religion, the family, and the customs which have evolved over the centuries.

CHAPTER 7

Religion and the Creoles

French culture and Roman Catholicism have always gone hand in hand. Today, even though New Orleans has become Americanized and the Catholic tradition is not as strong as it once was, the city remains one of the centers of Catholicism in the United States. Much of this strength is due to the Creoles, although they constitute only about one third of the Catholic black population of New Orleans. One of the provisions of the French Code Noir of 1724 was that all slaves and all free people of color should be of the Catholic faith; the Creoles' association with the Roman Catholic Church began then. Soon, devout Catholicism would be one of the white traditions imitated by the Creoles in order to separate themselves from the slaves and other non-Creole Negroes, who paid lip service to Catholicism when they had to but leaned toward the Protestant faiths. Later, it would be a way to separate themselves also from the white Americans who flocked to New

Orleans after the Louisiana Purchase. The influx of Catholic refugees from Haiti helped to strengthen their ranks in this regard.

The Haitian refugees, however, also brought with them a group of beliefs and practices that were outlawed by the Catholic Church. This was the cult of vodou. The term "vodou" originated in Haiti, and it was there that the cult, which has its roots in African religion, developed. It is centered around the worship of an all-powerful and supernatural being, personified by a serpent. Below the all-powerful serpent being are lesser gods whose spirits are believed to inhabit living and inanimate objects, and to have the ability to see the past, foretell the future, and perform acts that will affect human beings. Their knowledge can be made known and their help requested only through a priest or a priestess, who presides over ceremonies and sells charms, potions, and other magical aids.

The most famous vodou priestess in Louisiana was Marie Laveau, a Creole. But the Creoles as a group never practiced vodou. The cult had its most immediate appeal to the slaves in Louisiana, both because of its roots in African religions and its emphasis upon drums and dance, and because of its adaptability to incorporate certain Catholic practices. But the Creoles were, first, too staunchly Catholic and, second, too concerned with maintaining their separateness from the slaves to embrace vodou.

For many years the Catholic Church in Louisiana was not strongly affected by the ups and downs of the Creoles' status. From the early 1700s until the end of the Reconstruction period in the late 1870s, whites, blacks, and Creoles worshiped in the same churches, took communion together, and were baptized together. In 1841, Haitian refugees founded St. Augustine Church, but it was built more out of a feeling of community among the immigrants than of a desire for separation of any kind—for many years both white and black refugees worshiped together there.

It was not until after Reconstruction, when the Jim Crow laws had been firmly laid down, that nonwhite Catholics in New Orleans found themselves deterred from attending their traditional places of worship and thus forced to build separate churches. Whites often refused to allow anyone with black blood into the churches, and the Catholic Church, sadly fearful of the vengeful whites who held sway, encouraged the creation of churches for blacks alone. The Creoles hotly protested this further step toward lumping them together with other colored people. In 1895, St. Catherine's was opened for worship by Catholics of color, but Creoles who belonged to exclusively Creole congregations continued to go to their own churches. They did the same when, in 1909, St. Joan of Arc was established.

It was possible, always, to go to a biracial church—the old St. Louis Cathedral, St. Augustine Church, and a few others remained open to all—and many Creoles attended these. However, when Corpus Christi was built in 1916 in the heart of the Creole community, it immediately became an almost wholly Creole church. The Creoles did not really mind attending a separate church as long as they were almost exclusively by themselves. Even though segregation in the Catholic Church in Louisiana is no longer legal under either civil or church law, separate Negro churches have been in existence long enough to maintain the old pattern. Many of these churches have become centers of religious, educational, and social activity in their communities, and such ties are not apt to be broken simply because the parishioners now have the right to attend a white church.

Today there are some fifteen Negro Catholic churches in New Orleans. Corpus Christi parish has the largest Creole membership. It has grown so much since 1916 that it has split into several branch churches—St. Raymond's, St. David's, and Epiphany. Today, Corpus Christi is the largest Negro Roman Catholic church parish in the United States, and is second only to Abyssinian Baptist Church in New York City as the largest black church of any denomination in the country. In keeping with the importance of the Catholic faith in the Creole culture,

Corpus Christi plays a very central role in the Creole community. It operates a kindergarten, a grammar school, and a community center as well as a variety of other social and charitable organizations and activities. On Sundays, masses begin at 6 A.M. and continue every hour until noon; each mass is attended by throngs, for the majority of Creoles go to mass regularly on Sunday. The color consciousness that remains among the Creoles is evident in the attendance at these masses. The eleven-o'clock mass is called the "Creole" mass, as it is the service favored by the fair-skinned Creoles; darker-skinned Creoles usually go to earlier services.

Observing Holy Days of Obligation, receiving the sacraments, worshiping saints, celebrating feast days—all of these Catholic practices and obligations are characteristic of the Creole faith. Besides Christmas and Easter, All Saints' Day and St. Joseph's Day are the most frequently celebrated religious holidays. All Saints' Day, the feast commemorating the souls of the dead, is traditionally celebrated in France and also in Latin American countries. On that day in the fall, Catholics visit the graves of their loved ones, taking their meal right at the cemetery and talking with others who have come to spend the day at the tombs of their families. St. Joseph's Day is not as important in France or Latin America as it is among the Creoles of New Orleans—and in fact the Creoles seem to have adopted the observance from the Italians living near the Creole community. Falling during Lent, it is a night on which the lenten rules of abstinence are relaxed. The Creoles would not like to admit that their observance of St. Joseph's Day was adopted from a non-Creole group; but one can easily imagine them watching the Italians feasting and celebrating right in the middle of Lent—and deciding that, as good Catholics, they should be celebrating St. Joseph's Day, too!

The Creoles owe much to the Roman Catholic Church. The records of St. Louis Cathedral are a testimony of their family history; non-Creole Negroes can only guess at their past, for no church cared to record the births, marriages, and deaths of their forefathers. And in times of great discrimination or when the Creoles' special status has been otherwise threatened, the Church has served as a major focal point of the inwardly turned Creole community.

CHAPTER 8

The Creole Family

Next to the French culture and Roman Catholicism, the family is the most important factor in the continuing unique status of the Creoles. Indeed, without the family to stress the values and mores of this French Catholic culture it would soon fade away.

It might seem to some, after reading about the quadroon balls and the *plaçage* system of the eighteenth and nineteenth centuries, that the Creoles hardly had an opportunity to develop a true family system until the late 1870s, after Reconstruction, when segregation brought about an end to open relationships between white men and women of color. But it should be remembered that even as early as the period of Spanish rule, there existed a class of *gens de couleur* who owned property and slaves or who were skilled craftsmen—who hired tutors for their children or sent their children to schools in France. These were free men of color who had married free women of color and who disapproved of interracial unions, chiefly because they were outside the Church. Their family relationships were the forerunners of the Creole family system today, for it was these early families who adopted and continued the French Catholic customs and attitudes of the whites of French heritage.

As among all groups, economic status usually determines the size of the Creole family, the roles of mother and father, and so on. Lower-class Creole families are generally large, with many children and often grandparents or aunts and uncles living together. Sometimes the wife is the sole provider of the family, while the unemployed husband stays home and does many of the household chores. In such cases, she has considerable authority: being the provider, she is also the decision maker. If the husband has a job the wife usually stays home and has little authority. Thus, in the lower-class family the roles of husband and wife tend to be reversible.

Large, too, are middle-class Creole families, although they are not usually as large as lower-class families. Reversal of roles is rare among the middle class. The husband is generally the lord of the house, the decision maker, while the wife is expected to take care of the house and the children, with the husband functioning as sole provider.

Though generally larger than upper-class families in other groups, upper-class Creole families are

smaller than middle- or lower-class Creole families.
The wife is much more likely to have a job or other
interest outside the home than the middle-class wife.
Since she works because she wants to rather than
because she has to, she and her husband tend to be
fairly equal in authority. As a matter of fact, compared with his nineteenth-century role—at least his
social role—the upper-class Creole husband's authority has increased. In the golden age of the 1830s to
1850s, when Creoles of wealth owned boxes in the
second tier of the Théâtre d'Orléans, it was accepted
form for the women to flirt with the white men in the
first tier. The Creole men, however, were not so much
as to look at the first tier; yet despite this unequal
social situation, they were reported to have been
models of politeness and solicitude toward their
women.

Although class differences are found throughout
the various areas of family life, certain attitudes and
practices are common among all classes. Families are
generally very close, and there is much visiting among
relatives, including second and even third cousins.
Often a grandparent or other relative lives with the
family. Families engage in many activities together,
particularly those that have a religious meaning; at
times of birth, christening, first communion, marriage, and death all the aunts and uncles and cousins
who can possibly make it attend the occasion.

Christenings are very important affairs. Usually taking place a few weeks after the birth of the infant, they involve feasting and dancing in an elaborate, costly, and long-lasting celebration. Those relatives chosen as godparents are deeply honored and take their duties very seriously.

A child's first communion and, later, his confirmation are also festive occasions, with a huge breakfast following the ceremony. Hot rice cakes—*cala tout chaud*—are traditionally served. After the breakfast, the family sets out to call upon other families in the community in which children have just received first communion or been confirmed in the Church.

When a family member dies, a special effort is made by all the relatives to attend the funeral, no matter how far they must travel. The French custom of holding the funeral in the home used to be followed faithfully, although now more and more families are using funeral parlors. Relatives attending usually stay in the home all night, and although the activities surrounding the funeral have a solemn air, there is pleasure in being reunited with distant loved ones.

The Creole nuclear family—mother, father, and children, perhaps also a grandmother or an aunt—is very close-knit; many hours of the week are spent in joint pursuits. Meals are eaten together, from breakfast through dinner if possible. Evenings, too, are generally spent together, whether quietly at home or at a church or community function. On Sunday the entire family attends mass and then visits older relatives. Before the automobile, the entire family would go for a Sunday stroll after mass, but this practice has all but disappeared.

Children are very much loved in the Creole family, and when an infant is born the entire community is invited to call and congratulate the lucky

parents and to drink a glass of *orgeat*—the milk of almonds mixed with orange-flower water—to the health of the "little angel sent from heaven." Although they take great interest in their children, even selecting their companions, Creole parents are very strict. They demand obedience and respect; impoliteness or bad manners are punished. Daughters seem to be favored, which is neither a French nor an American tradition, but one of the few Creole attitudes that are closer to those of non-Creole Negroes. Perhaps this

is because Creole women, like non-Creole Negro women, have traditionally found greater opportunities for social, economic, and educational advancement than have the men.

Most families still expect children, both sons and daughters, to remain at home until they are married. If a young person expresses an interest in getting his own apartment or moving to another city, his reasons are immediately suspect. There is strong social pressure to marry within the community, although parents today have less to say in the matter than formerly. Once the son or daughter is married, there is equally great pressure to settle in the community and to maintain childhood ties with family and friends. Not actually stated, but strongly implied, is that otherwise the young person will be denying his Creole heritage—a heritage still stressed by the majority of Creole parents. The sense of unique status has until very recently formed the basis of much of the teaching of Creole parents: a child had to have good manners because he was a Creole; Creoles did not associate with Negroes; a young person should not go to college, because he would forget his Creole ways and values.

Although it remains traditional in many ways, the Creole family is changing. It is impossible for the Creole community to insulate itself completely from the influences that surround it; and the greater the contact with the outside world, the greater the changes that will occur in the Creole culture. American attitudes about social class can be seen to be seeping into the minds of young Creoles, who care less about a friend's or prospective mate's family background than about the person. The American stress on education is also reflected in the desire of increasing numbers of young Creoles to go to college. Some Creole parents are even beginning to teach their children not to think of themselves as Creoles or blacks, but simply as Americans.

CHAPTER 9

Creole Education

While education is considered one of the most important determinants of social class among Americans at large, among the Creoles education is less important than family background, color, and moral conduct. Those who do value education tend to stress parochial school training, seeing it as a further means to instill the Creole Catholic culture. Even today few Creoles attend the public schools.

Creoles have a history of private education. Before the institution of public schooling in Louisiana, the majority of Louisianians, Creoles included, had little education of any kind. The upper classes were able to afford tutors and French schools for their children. When public schools were opened, free persons of color were originally barred from attending them; they were first admitted at the time the slaves were freed and were admitted also. Most Creoles refused to allow their children to attend school with the children of freedmen, and they opened small private schools of their own.

Today, the Creoles prefer to send their children to schools operated by their churches, among them Corpus Christi and Epiphany. They do so for several reasons: it is the rule of the Church; the children will be taught the Catholic faith at school as well as at home; the children will go to school with other Creoles. Of those Creole parents who do send their children to the public elementary school in the Creole community, many prefer that they continue in a Catholic high school. When the children reach high school age their parents become concerned with marriage prospects, and the desire that their children find Creole mates prompts the parents to scrape together the money to enter them in a high school predominantly attended by Creoles.

The two parochial high schools that Creoles attend are Xavier Prep, a coeducational school, and St. Augustine High School, a boys' school. Once, there was a girls' school, St. Mary's, located in the former Orleans Ballroom. Now this site is occupied by the Royal Bourbon Hotel. Some Creoles attend public high school, but they are in the minority there.

Although most Creoles feel it is important to finish high school, college enjoys considerably less regard. For one thing, education is not valued beyond that amount necessary for learning basic skills and concepts. For another, college is extremely suspect as an environment encouraging among young Creoles a rejection of the Creole way of life. Therefore, many Creole families actively discourage their children from going to college. Xavier University was founded in 1915 as an extension of Xavier Prep, and most Creoles who go to college go there; yet there are more non-Creole blacks than Creoles at Xavier. Creole young men tend to go into skilled crafts, which require an apprenticeship, not a college education. Creole young women, though encouraged somewhat more to go to college, tend to value marriage above a college education and often drop out early.

The Creole youth who remain at Xavier University most often associate with other Creoles, and the non-Creole black students also associate with their own; yet there is enough interaction and enough learning about the outside world so that the majority of college-educated Creoles do indeed forsake some aspects of their traditional way of life. They become professionals, continuing to mix with non-Creoles; they are more likely to send their children to public school; and they are inclined to teach their children that being an American is equally as prideful as being a Creole. Then, too, they are more likely to leave New Orleans for a city in the North or the West, where job opportunities will be greater than in the city of their birth, in which the white society still determines in large measure the kind of work they will do.

CHAPTER 10

Creole Occupations

Occupation is considered second only to personal fame as the *least* important determinant of social status among Creoles, and this attitude of course helps to account for the lack of importance they attach to education. Nevertheless, the fact that Creoles do not place a premium upon becoming a doctor or a lawyer does not mean that many are not proud of their occupations. Particularly those whose skills have been handed down in their families from generation to generation take great pride in their work, and its quality is recognized by all segments of the population.

Once, the Creoles monopolized many of the skilled trades in New Orleans. They almost exclusively controlled the mechanical arts, woodcrafts, and construction jobs such as masonry and ironwork; and it was they who built, under the Spanish, most of what is now the Old City. After the Louisiana Purchase, Irish and Italian immigrants as well as other newcomers challenged this monopoly, and now the Creoles control none of these trades. Their work, however, is still considered the best, and the majority of middle-class Creoles are still employed in construction.

Tradition plays an important role, as does the sense of community. Their local union halls, descendants of the old guild halls of the nineteenth and early twentieth centuries, continue to function as civic and social centers. The sense of history within these walls has an important impact upon the Creole carpenters, bricklayers, masons, painters, plasterers, and ironworkers who frequent them. The attraction of construction work is diminishing, however; some sons are forsaking the traditional occupations of their forefathers in favor of the clerical opportunities opened to them by the United States Postal Service and other civil service bodies since the end of World War II.

Other traditional occupations have declined because of technical advances. Cigar manufacturing was once a Creole-controlled industry. Especially before the industrial revolution and the beginning of mass production, many middle- and lower-class Creole homes were miniature factories where cigars were rolled by several members of the family. Sometimes the family set up a stand in front of their home to sell their wares; other times they sold the home-rolled cigars to a larger distributor. As the idea of mass production reached the cigar industry in Louisiana, factories rose, and then the Creoles went out to the factories to roll cigars. When cigar-rolling machines were invented, the industry ceased to be a primarily Creole occupation, but even today Creole women are favored as cigar machine operators.

Another former Creole line of work that has been taken over by machines is the shoemaking industry. In the days when shoes were handmade, a customer went to a shoemaker's shop, chose the wooden form, or last, closest to his foot size, and ordered a pair of shoes made to fit that last. Creoles were the foremost shoemakers in the city. But when shoe factories were established, most of the Creole shoemakers were put out of business. Although some Creoles continued to operate shoe repair shops, shoe manufacturing did not become a major New Orleans industry. Instead, it moved north, leaving the Creoles without jobs.

Clothing manufacture continues today as a Creole occupation, although it, too, is now a factory industry, and now the Creoles are not owners and workers both but simply workers. At one time, a majority of the Creole women who earned a living worked as seamstresses; and some were skillful enough to achieve the position of *modiste,* or fashionable seamstress. They operated their own shops, and the fashionable ladies of the city would go there with their catalogues depicting the latest styles from Paris, or perhaps pore over the catalogues in the *modiste*'s shop, and would then select fabric and order a dress. Several fittings were required: dressmaking, before the arrival of clothing factories, was a true art. Tailoring, or the making of men's clothing, was monopolized in turn by Creole men. The advent of the factories of course forced the closing of a majority of the *modiste* and tailoring shops, as had been the case with shoemaking shops and home cigar-rolling. But Creoles, especially Creole girls, now form the bulk of the workers in New Orleans clothing factories. The only two men's-clothing factories in New Orleans are located in the Creole community.

Today, the majority of the occupations in which Creoles engage are still in the construction field. Creoles who have gone to college or who are in the upper classes are well represented among teachers and construction contractors. But some Creoles can be found in nearly every occupational group, including lawyers, insurance and real estate agents, radio and television repairmen, and secretaries. No longer are any occupations dominated exclusively by Creoles, but then again, no longer are most occupations closed to Creoles because they are nonwhite. Even some of those positions still supposedly unavailable to nonwhites, such as high elective or appointive public offices, have been infiltrated by Creoles who are passing—either permanently or just for eight hours a day.

CHAPTER 11

Creoles in Politics

The history of the Creoles in politics closely parallels that of their legal status in relation to both the whites and the blacks of New Orleans. That history really begins with the Louisiana Purchase, for prior to 1803 politics, as we know it, did not exist. In the seventeenth and eighteenth centuries, under the French and the Spanish, all power resided in far-off European rulers and in their selected representatives, the French and Spanish governors.

The Louisiana Purchase and the American take-over of Louisiana resulted in the first entry of the Creoles into politics—for the Americans soon abolished, legally, the Creoles' separate status. Although the terms of the Louisiana Purchase had granted all free people the right of suffrage, once the Americans were in power they modified these terms and restricted the suffrage to whites. This restriction gave rise to the first Creole political activity. The Creoles attempted to regain their voting rights; thus their first foray into politics was a defensive action. It failed, and from that time until the Civil War the Creoles watched, powerless, as one by one their other rights were taken away and as more and more their *legal* status did not really differ from that of other free people of color.

The Civil War, ironically, laid the way for the second advance of the Creoles into politics. Americans have long had mixed feelings about democracy. When democracy fits in with their plans to gain wealth, they are very democratic. When democracy does not fit in with those plans, they conveniently forget about it in some respects. When both North and South were chiefly agricultural, few Americans felt very guilty about owning slaves to work the fields or about treating nonwhites as something less than human beings. But then the North turned from agriculture to industry, and required not just labor but at least partially skilled labor. Slavery was now no longer profitable for the North, and thus it died out there. At the same time, the North began to rethink its attitudes toward democracy: if all men were created equal, then slaves should be equal, too, and shame on the South for continuing to practice slavery. Of course slavery was not the main reason for the War Between the States; more serious was the new industrialization of the North versus the continued agriculturalism of the South. Freeing the

southern slaves was not the issue; bringing the South
into line with the economic thinking of the North
was. That issue just happened to involve the North's
rethought ideas about democracy.

The war was fought and the North won, and
suddenly the Creoles found themselves in a compara-
tively powerful political position. Although they were
considered in the same category as other free Negroes, including the newly freed slaves—a status they
did not like—as educated and propertied people they
were also considered automatic leaders of the Negro
race in the age of the "new equality." Through
Reconstruction the North was determined to shame
the South—to allow Negroes to rule it, to set up a
democracy that did not exist even in the North. Even
before Reconstruction, in 1863, the Creoles had seen
the fresh possibility of political power and had asked
the governor of Louisiana to give them the right of
suffrage. Their plea had reached President Abraham
Lincoln and had caused even Lincoln to change his
opinion that the vote should belong only to white
people. That decision caused the Creoles to feel a
sense of power that they had not felt in a long time.

During the period of Reconstruction, when the
North was free to impose its ideas of democracy upon
a resistant South, Creoles participated actively in
politics. They helped to form the Republican Party in
Louisiana, helped to frame the new state constitution

of 1868, served as state senators and representatives
and even as state officials. They played a role in
positive changes that could have had a permanent
effect upon the South—if the North had not become
tired and decided that a South without democracy
was needed more than a South with democracy. In
exchange for the produce and the markets of the
South, the North decided again to ignore democracy,
and in the process sold out all southern people of
color, including the Creoles.

After the Reconstruction period, whites resisted
any ideas of democracy as it related to nonwhites,
and retaliation against some Creoles occurred. Gone
was any hint of separate status from other free people
of color or former slaves. Many Creoles left Louisiana. Others, unwilling or unable to leave, remained to
face the worst discrimination and segregation that
Creoles had ever endured. They formed groups like
the Comité des Citoyens to fight the creeping segregation; but there was no stopping it. After 1915, the
political participation of the Creoles came, essentially, to a standstill.

Political activity did not surface again until just
before World War II, and then it was an aspect of the
general American black political awareness. The
Creoles had realized that, politically at least, they
could no longer remain a separate class somewhere
between white and black; if they wanted any political

power at all, they would have to cast their lot with other blacks. Thus they began to take action beyond the concerns of their own community and cooperated with the Negro cause for political reasons—and they did not leave when the going got rough. Creoles became the presidents of local chapters of the National Association for the Advancement of Colored People and the Congress of Racial Equality, the prominent lawyers in civil rights suits, the editors of the most militant black weeklies.

And yet—just like non-Creole blacks, the Creoles still show a relatively lower voter registration than whites. Creole political organizations are working together to bring the Creole and the Negro voting population to the proportionate mark. In politics, especially, the Creole cannot afford to remain aloof. Though his unique identity may not depend upon his political assets, his status as a nonwhite in New Orleans does. Thus, his political activity will grow and grow until he either achieves true equality or is again relegated categorically to second-class citizenship for the economic purposes of white society.

SECTION III
Some Creole Contributions

CHAPTER 12

The Creole Language

The Creole language developed when African slaves learned French in order to communicate with their masters, as well as with one another. The language that evolved among the slaves was a very simplified French, ungrammatical and laughable to those Frenchmen who had heard their own language from birth and had been taught its grammar in school. But the slaves' type of French could not have been otherwise.

First, the Frenchmen from whom they heard the language most often were either of the lower class or men who made a point of speaking very simplified French to the slaves. Second, many of the French sounds were completely foreign to the slaves—for instance, the French *"r,"* which is also one of the hardest sounds for an American learning French today to pronounce. The slaves said *"vend"* for *"vendre,"* and *"neg"* for *"nègre."* Many of the French hard consonants also proved difficult for them, accustomed as they were to the softer sounds of their African languages. Sometimes, therefore, they simply substituted an African word with a similar meaning. Third, the grammatical structure of the French language was very different from that of the African languages; and thus, like other people who learn a foreign language without going to school, the slaves tended to apply the rules of their native tongues to French.

The result of these differences and difficulties was an Afro-French patois which eventually became almost a language in its own right and was passed on from generation to generation. Proof that it is indeed almost a true language is the similarity between Creole in Louisiana and the idioms of Haiti and other West Indian areas where French influence is predominant.[8]

As the number of free people of color grew, and as they became more and more educated and careful to imitate white ways, they stopped speaking the Creole language and spoke proper French. Yet they retained a pride in their former characteristic speech and began to resent the fact that this Afro-French language was called the "Creole dialect." New terms, such as Gombo and Baragouin, arose among them to describe it. Whatever it was called, it was widely spoken among Creoles of the lower classes, and in fact its soft, lilting sound was so pleasing that many whites of the lower classes came to speak it among themselves. Certain words even crept into the speech of the upper classes—the best known of which was *gombo. Gombo* comes from the African word *kingombo,* the word for okra. As okra is almost always used in Creole soups, *gombo* came also to mean "mixture." Thus, the language developed by the slaves in Louisiana became, by extension, Gombo. Other words were *bé,* short for the French *bébé,* and *ché,* short for the French *cher*—both terms of affection; and *gris-gris,* originally a magic charm, that came to mean almost any kind of luck.

Around World War I, the Creole dialect began to die out quickly, for the American language and American culture were becoming too strong. More American words were used, and the Creoles' speech became less rhythmical. Even the dialect street cries of the various *marchandes* and special service workers changed. The chimney sweep, dressed all in black, his top hat crumpled, had formerly chanted in Creole:

Ramoné	Sweep
la chiminée!	the chimney!
C'est li tems, oui,	It's time, yes,
C'est l'hiver, oui.	It's winter, yes.
Ramoné ci,	Sweep here,
Ramoné la,	Sweep there,
Ramoné li,	Sweep it,
de haut en bas.	from top to bottom.
Ramoné!	Sweep!

After World War I, the chimney sweep was more likely to cry:

Rami, rami, rami, ramineau,
here's de chim-il-lo-o sweeper!
Chunka lunka chunka lunka chunka lou ou ou,
here's de chim-il-lo-o sweeper!
Ramineau!! Ramineau!!!!!![9]

Today, only older Creoles can remember the language, although certain French and Creole words remain in currency: *guignon,* meaning "bad luck"; *bamboucher,* "to have a good time"; *lagniappe,* "something extra"; *machouquer,* "to talk all the time." But generally, although there is still a slight French accent to many Creoles' speech, most learn French only in school, just like other Americans.

CHAPTER 13

Creole Music

Like other aspects of the Creole culture, Creole music was influenced chiefly by French music; but also like the other aspects, certain African and West Indian influences were brought to the French forms to make Creole music distinctively Creole. These secondary influences were more prominent in lower-class Creole culture than among the middle class; and in upper-class Creole music, they hardly existed at all.

The upper-class Creoles favored French classical music and French opera. If their sons desired a career in music, they were sent to Paris for instruction or, if that was not possible, to music teachers who had been trained in Paris. Music was an accepted career in upper-class Creole circles, and by the late 1830s there was a Negro Philharmonic Society, with more than a hundred members, in New Orleans.

In the music of lower-class Creoles, the African and West Indian influences were clearly heard. African rhythms softened even the harshest French marching tunes, and African, West Indian, and

Creole humor enlivened the French sentimentality. The spoken Creole French of the lower classes, softer than the language of the whites or upper-class Creoles, was especially pleasing to the ear when put to music:

> *Pov' piti Momzel Zizi,*
> *Pov' piti Momzel Zizi,*
> *Li gagin bobo, bobo*
> *Dans so piti kèr à li.*[10]

The lower-class Creoles loved to make up songs, about anything—but Creole French set to music was not so pleasing if you happened to be the object of a Creole taunt song:

> *Ah! Toucoutou, yé connin vou,*
> *Vou cé tin Morico;*
> *Na pa savon qui tacé blanc*
> *Pou blanchi vou lapo.*

Ah, Toucoutou, we all know you,
You're just a passing white!
There is no hope to find a soap
To make your skin like white.[11]

Even the street cries of Creole vendors were musical, such as that of the woman who sold sweet-potato cakes:

Bel pain pa-tate, bel pain pa-tate
Madame, ou-lé-ou le bel pain pa-tate![12]

Music was everywhere. The Creole craft guilds each had a marching band to provide music for the dances, picnics, and parades which these craftsmen's associations sponsored. The musicians dressed in French military uniforms and would often parade through the downtown Creole community. Crowds would follow them—not just because there was a parade but because the music they made was not

quite like that of a white French band; there were extra beats, a faster, sometimes surprising rhythm.

The funeral of a member of one of these craft associations was a grand affair, with all expenses paid by the guild. The guild's band would accompany the funeral procession to and from the cemetery. The music was very solemn on the way to the cemetery, but it took on a slightly lighter tone on the way back. There were several reasons for this change. For one, the entire family was together, perhaps for the first time in many years; for another, the Creoles were strong Catholics, and they believed their deceased loved one was now safely in the hands of the Lord. As the years passed, the music on the way back became so merry that large crowds were attracted; and many Creoles stopped the custom, feeling that it was undignified for a Catholic funeral.

Among middle- and lower-class Creoles, a musical career was not considered a proper one, and so music remained an everyday popular activity and was not meant to be innovative or influential upon the music of other groups. Nevertheless it was—for without meaning to do so, the Creoles helped to bring about the birth of American jazz.

In the founding of jazz, New Orleans Creoles and New Orleans blacks collaborated. This could have happened only after the Reconstruction period and the segregation laws of the 1890s. The Creoles, who had enjoyed a status separate from the New

Orleans blacks, suddenly found themselves pushed into the black culture. For a time they hoped for a return of their old recognition, but when that did not happen, many, especially in the lower classes, accepted at least some aspects of the black culture. One of those aspects was music; and in the area of music both Creoles and blacks gained much from each other. The Creoles brought with them a valuable knowledge of the structure of music, of the various musical "times"; they brought the tradition of French love songs. These things fitted in well with the black characteristics—the emotion of "blues" songs, the spontaneity and freedom of a music that had always been felt rather than taught.

The blending of the two musical traditions appeared first, and perhaps most famously, in the funeral marches. New Orleans blacks had watched the Creole funeral marches with interest, but not until the gap between Creole and black had been lessened by law did they adopt the custom. The merry music of the return march from the cemetery began to be called "ragtime." Within a few more years, the musicians in the funeral marches had begun to improvise ragtime in dance halls and cafés, and jazz was truly on its way to becoming the first (and as yet only) native American musical form.

Although non-Creole Negroes would eventually take jazz to its highest development, several Creoles became true "jazz greats." "Jelly Roll" Morton, one of the greatest jazzmen of all time, was a Creole, whose real name was Ferdinand LaMenthe. Other greats were Kid Ory, Sidney Bechet, Papa Celestin, and Alphonse Picou. All were brave men who refused to listen to their Creole parents' criticisms that jazz sounded too much like the music of uptown Negroes, and that a career in music was not proper.

By World War I, jazz had left New Orleans, forced out by those who saw it as music played by unsavory characters in murky, crime-ridden places. But in being forced out, jazz had to find new places to go; and today it is known and loved all over the world. Those who know it well understand how great a part the Creoles of New Orleans played in its birth.

CHAPTER 14

Creole Proverbs and Superstitions

One of the most enjoyable things to learn about any group of people is their proverbs and superstitions: those sayings and beliefs, handed down from generation to generation, that make up such a large part of folklore the world over. The Creoles of color have a rich store of such folklore—some borrowed from the New Orleans French, some brought from Africa and the West Indies, and some a blend of these influences.

Creole superstitions do not seem to contain many African influences but rather are very European; in the nineteenth century the white French shared the same superstitious beliefs. Today those whites of French heritage in New Orleans no longer hold these beliefs, and it is the Creoles of color who carry on the tradition. Yet even the Creoles do not believe these superstitions anymore; they just like to remember them as something from the past. These are some Creole superstitions:

Cooking cabbage on New Year's means money for all.

If a man is the first to cross the threshold on a Monday morning it is good luck for the household.

If your left eye itches, you are going to get a whipping or get into trouble.

If a baby looks in a mirror before teething, he will take a long time cutting his teeth. He may also become cross-eyed.

If someone drops a fork, a hungry woman is coming to visit; if someone drops a knife, a hungry man is coming.

If you sprinkle salt on two matches, it will stop raining.

If a dog is howling outside, look out the window to see which way his head is pointing. If it points up, it means fire; if his head points down, it means death.

If an unwanted guest comes to visit, place a broom in a shoe and hide it behind a door, and the guest will leave; sprinkle salt and pepper on the doorsill, and he will never return.[13]

Unlike Creole superstitions, Creole proverbs show many African influences, and many are in fact direct translations. There is a timeless quality about a proverb—that mother wit, handed down from old to young, that says so much about life in a few words. Though the world may change, life stays pretty much the same, and proverbs never really die. It is likely that remembering African proverbs helped the slaves survive being forcibly uprooted and taken to an alien land; and that new proverbs, developed to meet the new situation, were used to teach the generations to come. These are some Creole proverbs:

Even the monkey finds his child beautiful.

A beautiful *tignon* does not make a beautiful woman of color.

The fox does not reason with the chicken.

Great to speak, little to do. (He who talks a lot does nothing.)

Ox who comes first always drinks clear water.

When the tree falls, the goat climbs it.

When one is very hungry, one does not peel the sweet potato.

Set your type, and then read it before you go. (Know what you are going to say before you say it.)

The best swimmer is often drowned.

With fine clothes one goes everywhere.[14]

CHAPTER 15

Creole Cooking

New Orleans cooking is famous throughout the world, and much of its fame is due to generations of Creole cooks. The French brought with them their fine tradition of sophisticated cookery and carefully taught it to their slaves. During the thirty-odd years that the Spaniards ruled the colony, the Spanish love for spicy foods influenced the French cooking habits. The slave cooks harmonized the two traditions, adding something of their own, as well as certain elements from West Indian cooking, to create a cuisine unequaled in its variety and richness of flavor. Throughout the world, it is known as Creole cooking.

Creole soups are among the most famous dishes: rabbit soup, crawfish bisque, coconut soup served with powdered sugar, jambalaya. Gombo, native to New Orleans, is the supreme pride. It can be made with chicken or turkey, squirrel or rabbit, crabs or shrimp, fresh oysters or diced ham; but it is always very highly seasoned, and it is always served on dry, flaky rice. Court bouillon is another favorite. Its basis is a fish called *poisson rouge*—red snapper—which has a red spot on the tail. Because of this spot, it is said to be the fish the Apostles brought to Jesus Christ when he performed the miracle of loaves and fishes. Creole cooks point out to the children that the red spot is "the mark of the Lord's hand."

The soups are always served with long loaves of hard, flaky French bread. In New Orleans restaurants diners are provided with metal scrapers to clean the bread crumbs from the tablecloth.

There are other famous dishes: oysters with spinach and bacon; turtle soup; roast oysters; sweetbreads, the soft, delicate gland from the throat of a suckling calf; *la médiatrice,* an oyster loaf filled with broiled or creamed oysters; *gâteau de roi,* a cake served on Twelfth Night, with hidden "jewels" or decorations of bonbons.

Of course, many who live in New Orleans cannot afford these dishes. The poor usually eat rice with red beans—it is said to be the dish for "strong and useful" men and women.

The Creole cooking tradition is so influential that even eggs laid in Louisiana are called Creole eggs, and Louisiana cabbage Creole cabbage. In New Orleans today, one can buy a hamburger or a hot dog or a bucket of Kentucky Fried Chicken; but one kind of food that probably will never become Americanized is Creole cooking.

The Future of
the Creoles

After a century and a quarter of resistance to Americanization, the Creoles of color realized that they could not remain totally separate from the rest of society, that they would have to change in some ways in order to function in that society. By the early years of the twentieth century, for example, they had essentially stopped speaking French, and now only a few French words remain in their speech.

After a century and a half of insistence upon being considered a class separate from other blacks, they have begun to realize that in some instances it is to their advantage to join and work with other blacks. In programs of civil rights and politics, unity within the entire black community is the only way for that community to wield any power. The Creoles, particularly young Creoles, have also been affected by the heightened pride and consciousness that have been felt by black Americans in the past decade, and have taken an interest in their black heritage. Gradually, the traditional Creole attitudes toward the color line are changing.

Yet with all these changes, the Creoles are not likely to forsake the unique qualities of their culture altogether, to blend in with and become indistinguishable from other blacks. Many of their traditions—the devout and pervasive Catholicism, close family ties, love of music and dancing, tendency to live and go to church and school together—remain strong. The Creole culture is a long-established and prideful one, and even the most progressive-thinking Creole is aware of and pleased about his special heritage.

Currently, Americans of all ethnic backgrounds are rediscovering and deriving pride in their cultural origins, coming to a new awareness of the fascinating variety and diversity of the people of America. It is a good atmosphere for the Creoles of New Orleans—a good time for them to continue advancing into the mainstream of American life while retaining enough of their traditions to survive as the unique group they are.

Notes

1. Lafcadio Hearn, *Leaves from the Diary of an Impressionist* (Boston: Houghton Mifflin, 1911), p. 5.

2. Charles L. Dufour, *Ten Flags in the Wind: The Story of Louisiana* (New York: Harper & Row, 1967), p. 86.

3. *Ibid.,* p. 130.

4. Charles E. Gayarré, *History of Louisiana*, vol. 2 (New Orleans: F. F. Hansel & Bro., 1903), p. 408.

5. Dufour, *Ten Flags*, p. 234.

6. *New Orleans Item*, December 20, 1880.

7. Edward Larocque Tinker, *Creole City* (New York: Longmans, Green & Co., 1953), pp. 271–275.

8. Jim Haskins and Hugh F. Butts, *The Psychology of Black Language* (New York: Barnes & Noble, 1973), pp. 34–35.

9. Edward Larocque Tinker, *Gombo: The Creole Dialect of Louisiana* (1936; reprinted from the *Proceedings of the American Antiquarian Society*, April 1935), pp. 29–30.

10. George W. Cable, "Creole Slave Songs," *Century Magazine*, vol. 31 (April 1886), p. 825.

11. Tinker, *Gombo*, p. 19. (English translation by the author.)

12. *Ibid.,* p. 29.

13. Roland Wingfield, "The Creoles of Color: A New Orleans Subculture" (M.A. thesis, Louisiana State University, 1961), pp. 224–225. (Paraphrased in some cases.)

14. J. Mason Brewer, *American Negro Folklore* (Chicago: Quadrangle Books, 1968), pp. 323–324; James F. Broussard, *Louisiana Creole Dialect* (Baton Rouge: Louisiana State University Press, 1942), pp. 33–36. (Paraphrased in some cases.)

Bibliography

ADAMS, BEN AVIS. "A Study of Indexes of Assimilation of the Creole People of New Orleans." M.A. thesis, Tulane University, 1939.

BREWER, J. MASON. *American Negro Folklore.* Chicago: Quadrangle Books, 1968.

BROUSSARD, JAMES F. *Louisiana Creole Dialect.* Baton Rouge: Louisiana State University Press, 1942.

CABLE, GEORGE W. *The Creoles of Louisiana.* New York: Charles Scribner's Sons, 1884.

————. "Creole Slave Songs." *Century Magazine,* vol. 31 (1886), 807–828.

————. *Old Creole Days.* New York: Charles Scribner's Sons, 1937.

————. "Who Are the Creoles?" *Century Magazine,* vol. 25, series 3 (1882–1883), 384–398.

CARTER, HODDING, et al., eds. *The Past as Prelude: New Orleans, 1718–1968.* New Orleans: Tulane University Press, 1968.

CASTELLANOS, HENRY C. *New Orleans as It Was.* New Orleans: L. Graham and Son, 1895.

"Creoles Outside the Color Line." *Literary Digest,* vol. 78 (1922), 59.

CURTIS, WARDON A. "The Creole Citizens of the United States." *Current History*, vol. 20 (1951), 636–639.

DUFOUR, CHARLES L. *Ten Flags in the Wind: The Story of Louisiana.* New York: Harper & Row, 1967.

EVANS, OLIVER. "Melting Pot in the Bayous." *American Heritage*, vol. 15 (1963), 30.

EVERETT, DONALD EDWARD. "Free Persons of Color in New Orleans, 1803–1865." Ph.D. dissertation, Tulane University, 1952.

FORTIER, ALCÉE. "A Few Words About the Creoles of Louisiana." Address delivered to Louisiana Education Association, 1892, at Tulane University. In series 1, circular 9, Louisiana Department of Education.

GAYARRÉ, CHARLES E. "The Creoles of History and the Creoles of Romance." Lecture delivered at Tulane University, Apr. 25, 1885. New Orleans: C. E. Hopkins.

———. *History of Louisiana.* New Orleans: F. F. Hansel & Bro., 1903.

HASKINS, JIM, and HUGH F. BUTTS, *The Psychology of Black Language.* New York: Barnes & Noble, 1973.

HEARN, LAFCADIO. *Creole Sketches.* Ed. by Charles Woodward Hutson. Boston: Houghton Mifflin, 1924.

———. *Leaves from the Diary of an Impressionist.* Boston: Houghton Mifflin, 1911.

HERSKOVITZ, MELVILLE J. *The Myth of the Negro Past.* Boston: Beacon Press, 1958.

KANE, HARNETT T. *Deep Delta Country.* Ed. by Erskine Caldwell. New York: Duell, Sloan & Pearce, 1944.

————. *Plantation Parade.* New York: William Morrow & Co., 1945.

KLEIN, SELMA LOUISE. "Social Interaction of the Creoles and Anglo-Americans in New Orleans, 1803–1860." M.A. thesis, Tulane University, 1940.

KNIFFEN, FRED B. *Louisiana: Its Land and People.* Baton Rouge: Louisiana University Press, 1968.

SAXON, LYLE. *Old Louisiana.* New York: Century Co., 1929.

SMITH, IRENE DIXON. "The Louisiana Creole in Fiction." M.A. thesis, Tulane University, 1926.

SMITH, T. LYNN. *The Population of Louisiana: Its Composition and Changes.* Louisiana State University and Agricultural and Mechanical College (Agricultural Experimental Stations) Louisiana Bulletin no. 293, 1937.

TINKER, EDWARD LAROCQUE. *Creole City.* Vols. 1, 2. New York: Longmans, Green & Co., 1953.

————. *Gombo: The Creole Dialect of Louisiana.* Reprinted from *Proceedings of the American Antiquarian Society, April 1935.* Worcester, Mass., 1936.

————. "Louisiana Gombo." *Yale Review*, vol. 21 (1932), 566–579.

TREGLE, JOSEPH G., JR. "Early New Orleans Society: A Re-appraisal." *Journal of Southern History*, vol. 18 (1952), 20–36.

WINGFIELD, ROLAND. "The Creoles of Color: A New Orleans Subculture." M.A. thesis, Louisiana State University, 1961.

Index

About the Author

James Haskins' many works include *Revolutionaries: Agents of Change*; *Resistance: Profiles in Nonviolence*; *The War and the Protest: Vietnam*; *A Piece of the Power: Four Black Mayors*; and *Profiles in Black Power*—all of which have been selected as notable children's books in the field of social studies. One of his books, *Diary of a Harlem Schoolteacher*, has been recorded for the blind. He has taught in New York City public schools as well as in various universities and colleges, and has been a guest on numerous radio and television programs. Mr. Haskins is currently working on books that reflect his wide range of interests: the Cotton Club, voodoo and hoodoo, special olympics, and youth rights. Born in Alabama, he lives in New York City.

About the Artist

Don Miller first began specializing in children's-book illustration after a successful career in commercial art. He is also a professional photographer; and his paintings, graphics, and sculpture have been widely exhibited. Born in the West Indies, he grew up and went to school in Montclair, New Jersey, where he now lives with his wife and two sons.